Interlibrary Loan Sharks and Seedy Roms

WITHDRAWN

To Ted

Interlibrary Loan Sharks and Seedy Roms

Cartoons from Libraryland

by

Benita L. Epstein

McFarland & Company, Inc., Publishers
Jefferson, North Carolina and London

British Library Cataloguing-in-Publication data are available

Library of Congress Cataloguing-in-Publication Data

Epstein, Benita L., 1950–
    Interlibrary library loan sharks and seedy roms : cartoons from
libraryland / by Benita L. Epstein.
        p.   cm.
    ISBN 0-7864-0465-5 (sewn softcover : 55# alkaline paper) ∞
    1. Libraries and readers — Caricatures and cartoons.   2. American
wit and humor, Pictorial.   I. Title.
NC1429.E68A4   1998
741.5'973 — dc21   97-40645
                                                                                    CIP

*No part of this book may be reproduced or transmitted in any form or by
any means, electronic or mechanical, including photocopying or recording,
or by any information storage and retrieval system, without permission in
writing from the publisher.*

Manufactured in the United States of America

McFarland & Company, Inc., Publishers
  Box 611, Jefferson, North Carolina 28640

Table of Contents

Foreword

by GraceAnne A. DeCandido

Benita Epstein and I have never met: we live and work on opposite sides of the country. We are soul mates, however, as Benita is with thousands of librarians, even though she is not a librarian. We are soul mates because Benita knows how to make us laugh: at ourselves, at our work, at our knotty quotidian problems, at gender and technology issues.

Her gift is one of deep empathy. The first time I saw one of her cartoons, I was astonished at how, with a pithy one-line caption and a multitude of squiggly lines, she seemed to go to the heart — and funny bone — of daily life in the library. *Wilson Library Bulletin* had a long history of publishing cartoons, and when I became its editor-in-chief in January 1993 I particularly wanted to nurture that history. Benita is one of the cartoonists whose work the editors and I chose most often, and whose cartoons were most often asked after for reprint.

Benita's career began with bugs: studying bugs and drawing bugs in the Entomology Department at the University of California at Davis. She went from there to a career in laboratory research, at which she excelled and for which she has copublished a dozen scientific papers. But she confessed, what she liked best was "taking half a day to make giant greeting cards for my fellow employees." When the last government grant ended and she was laid off for the fourth time, Benita, at 41, took a one-day cartooning class and two weeks later, sold her first cartoon.

Five years have passed. The trademark Benita style has appeared in 130 publications in print and on the world wide web, and dozens of greeting cards. From *American Scientist* to the *Saturday Evening Post*, from *Punch* to *Fantasy and Science Fiction*, Benita's cartoons reflect the milieu and gently tweak the sensibilities of their readers.

When Benita created cartoons for *Wilson Library Bulletin*, she read the magazine faithfully. Any idea or event that was explored in our news and feature pages was sure to find itself transformed into a madcap image with a zingy tagline a few weeks after its appearance. We counted on Benita to distill the difficult into the manageable; to make the love of words and the quest for information tangible; and to illumine the fragile compromises we make between family and workplace.

I love these cartoons, they comfort me and make me chuckle. You will love them too, and will share them with colleagues and paste copies on your terminals and bulletin boards and refrigerators. Enjoy!

GraceAnne Andreassi DeCandido lives in the Bronx, New York. She is the former editor-in-chief of Wilson Library Bulletin.

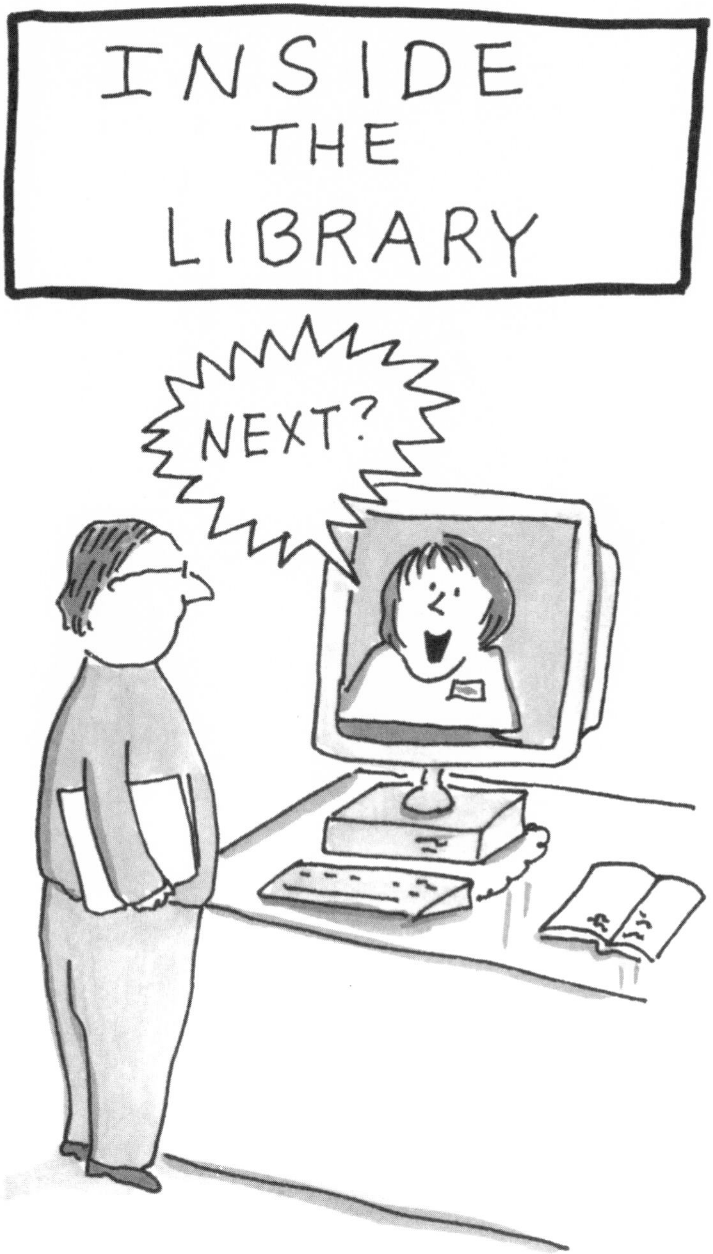
INSIDE THE LIBRARY
NEXT?

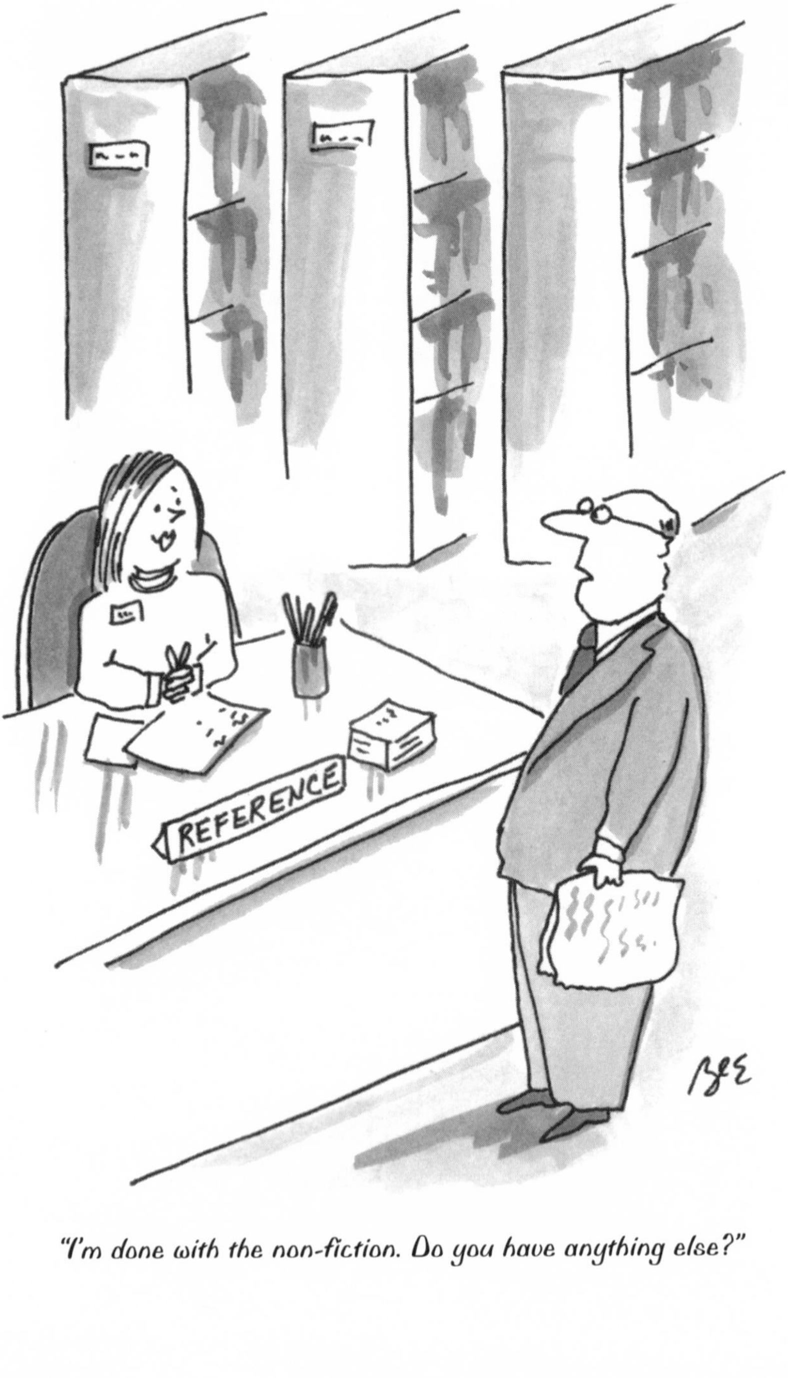
REFERENCE
BEE

"I'm done with the non-fiction. Do you have anything else?"

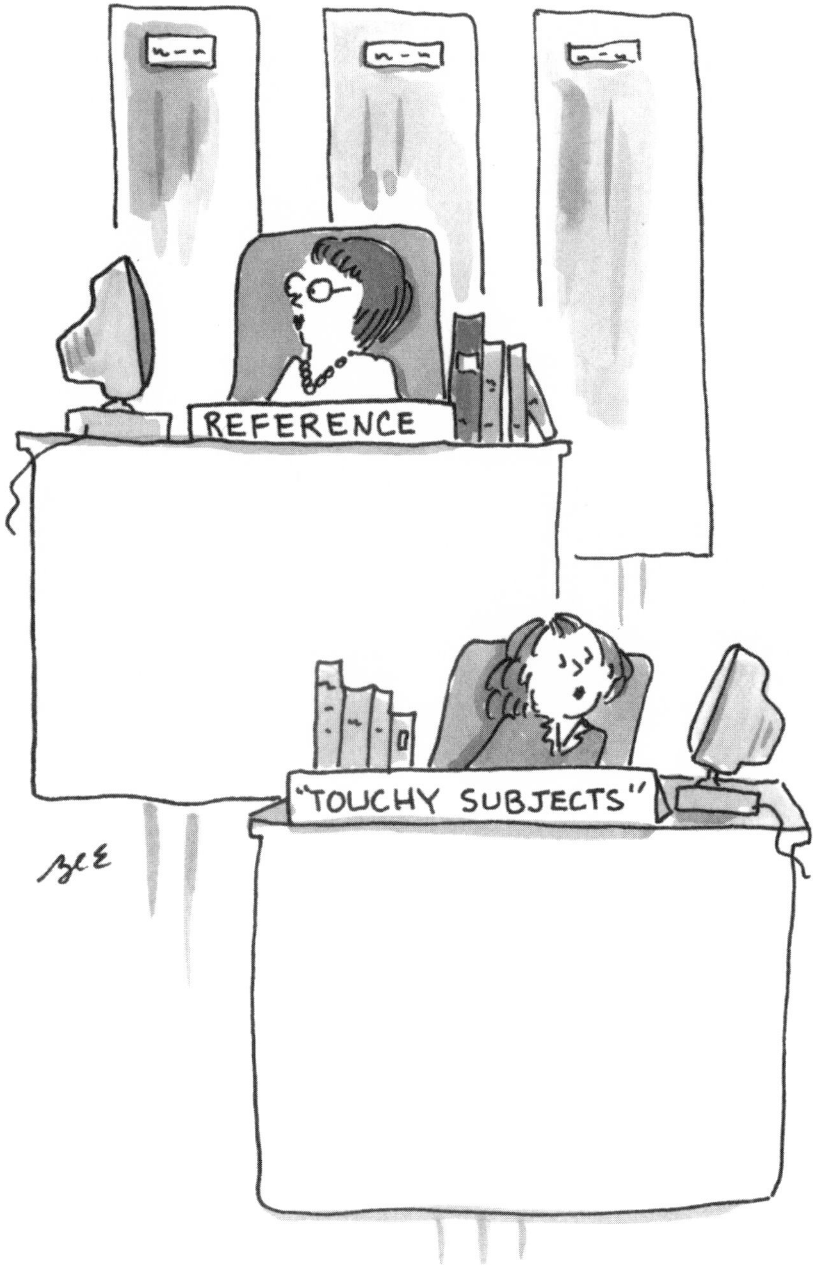
REFERENCE
"TOUCHY SUBJECTS"
ZEE

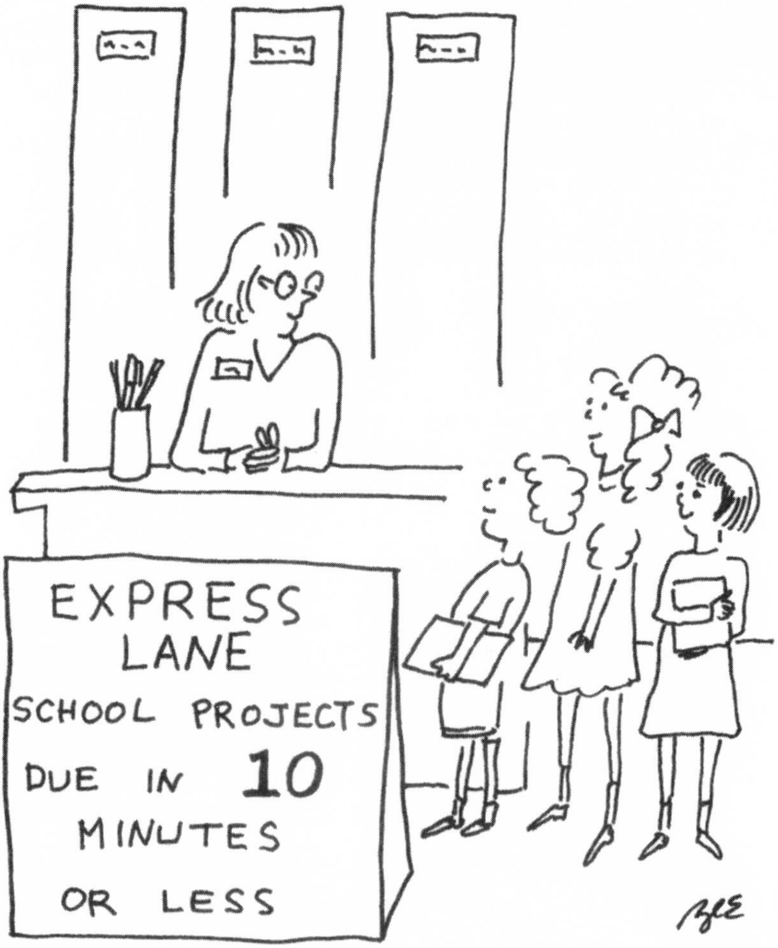
EXPRESS
LANE
SCHOOL PROJECTS
DUE IN 10
MINUTES
OR LESS

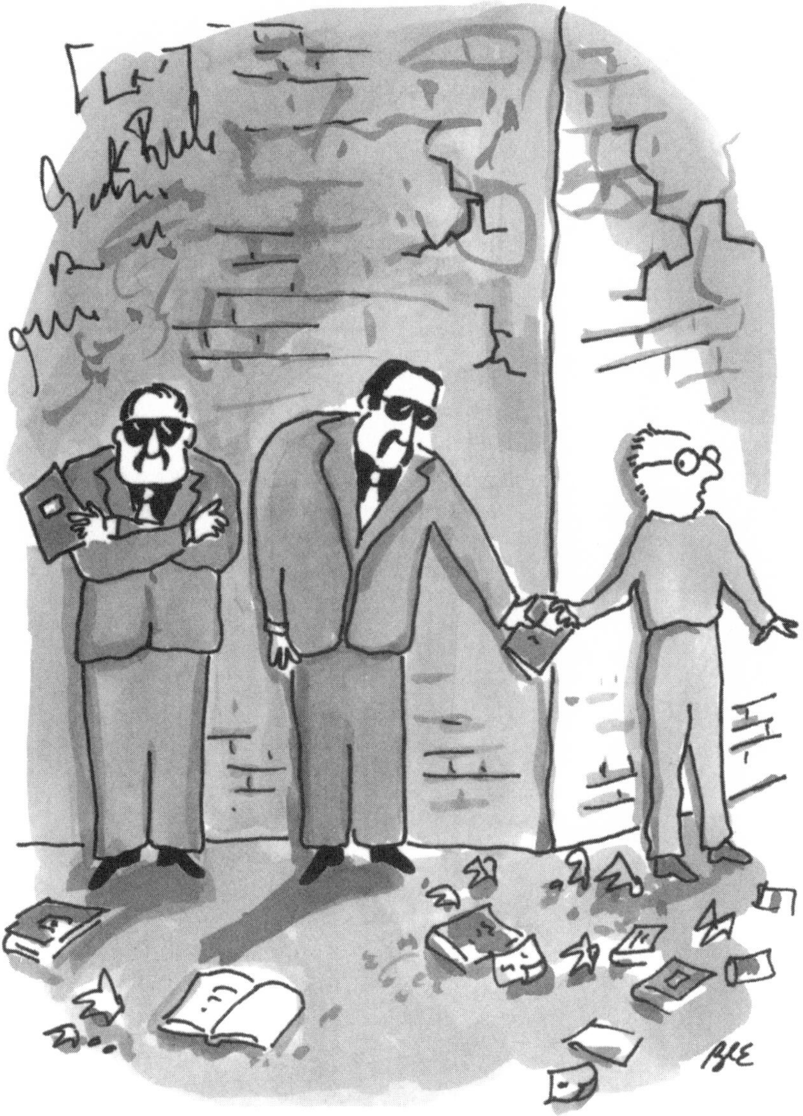

INTERLIBRARY LOAN SHARKS

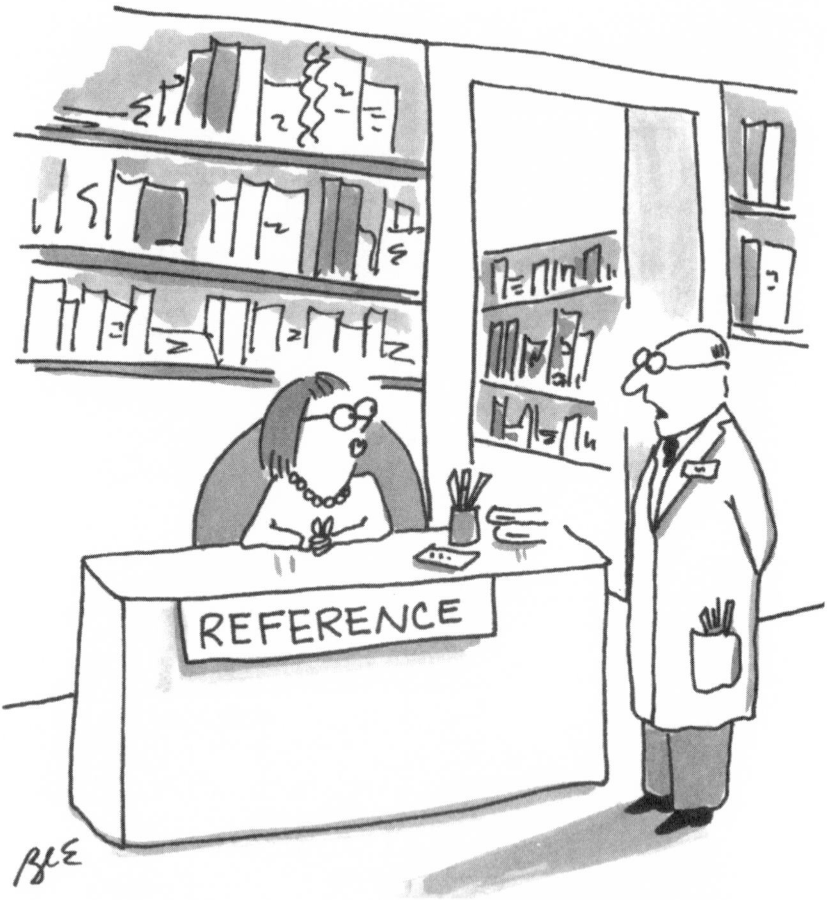
REFERENCE

"Where will I find the fine line between art and science?"

"I've come for the acidified books."

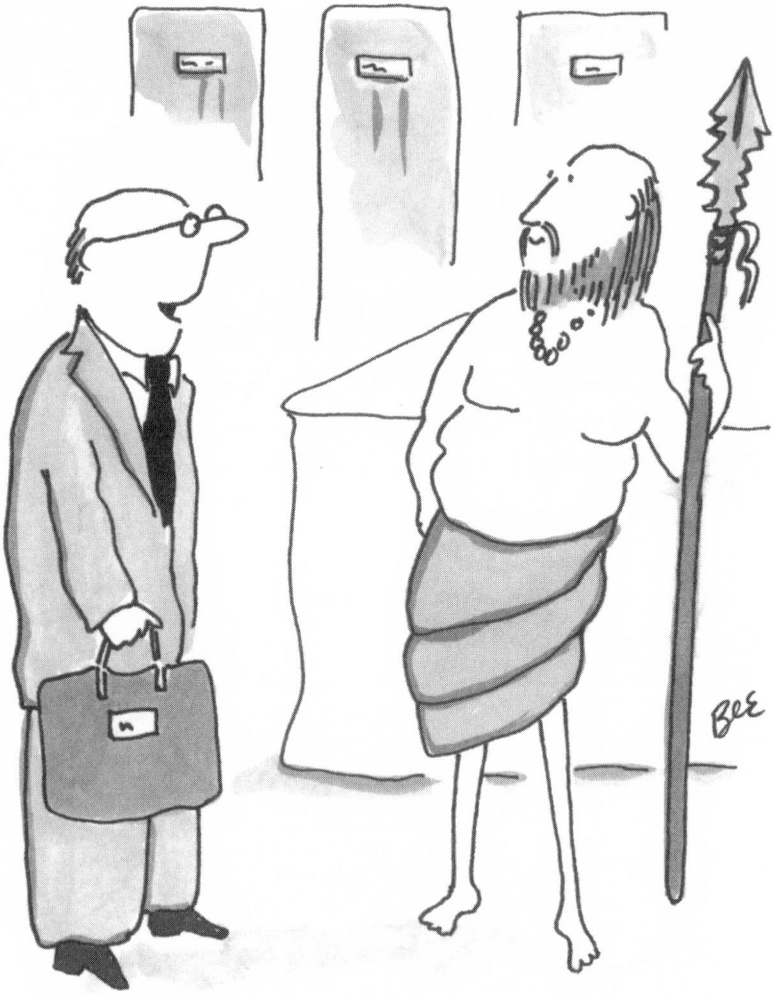
BEE

"When did you get back from your sabbatical?"

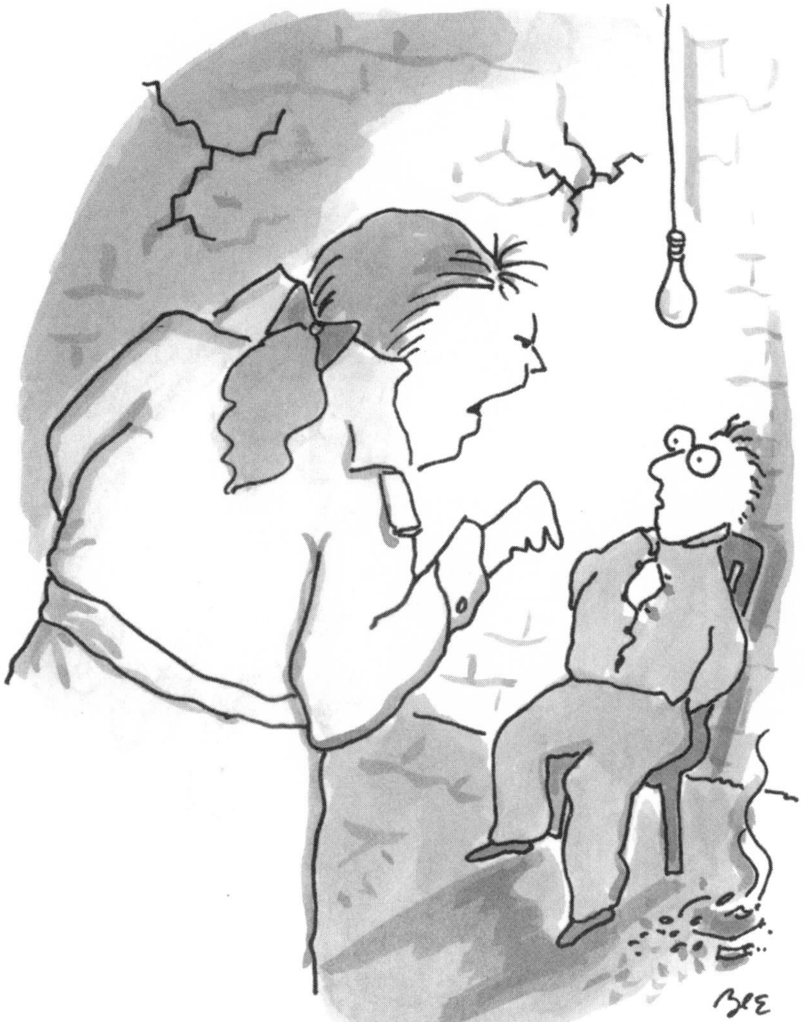
BEE

"I'm a librarian! It's my job to ask questions."

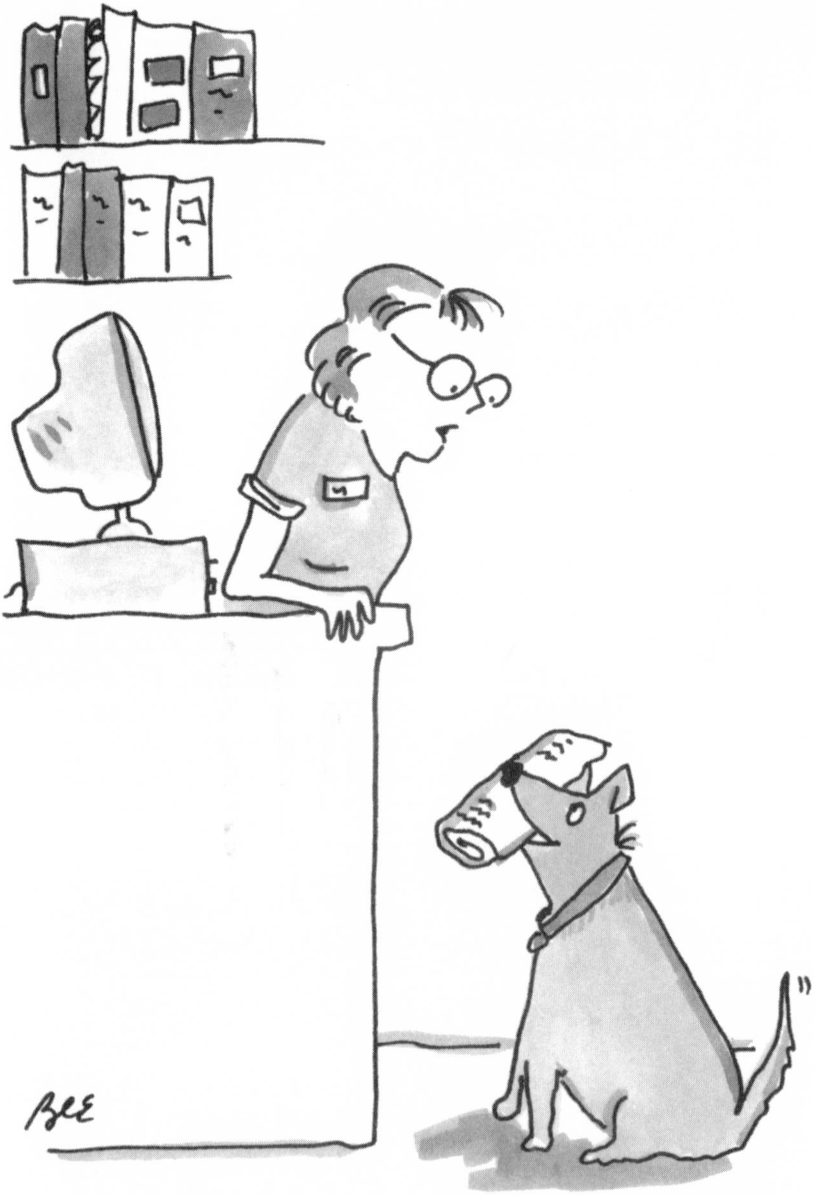

"You call yourself a retriever? I need 150,000 science abstracts."

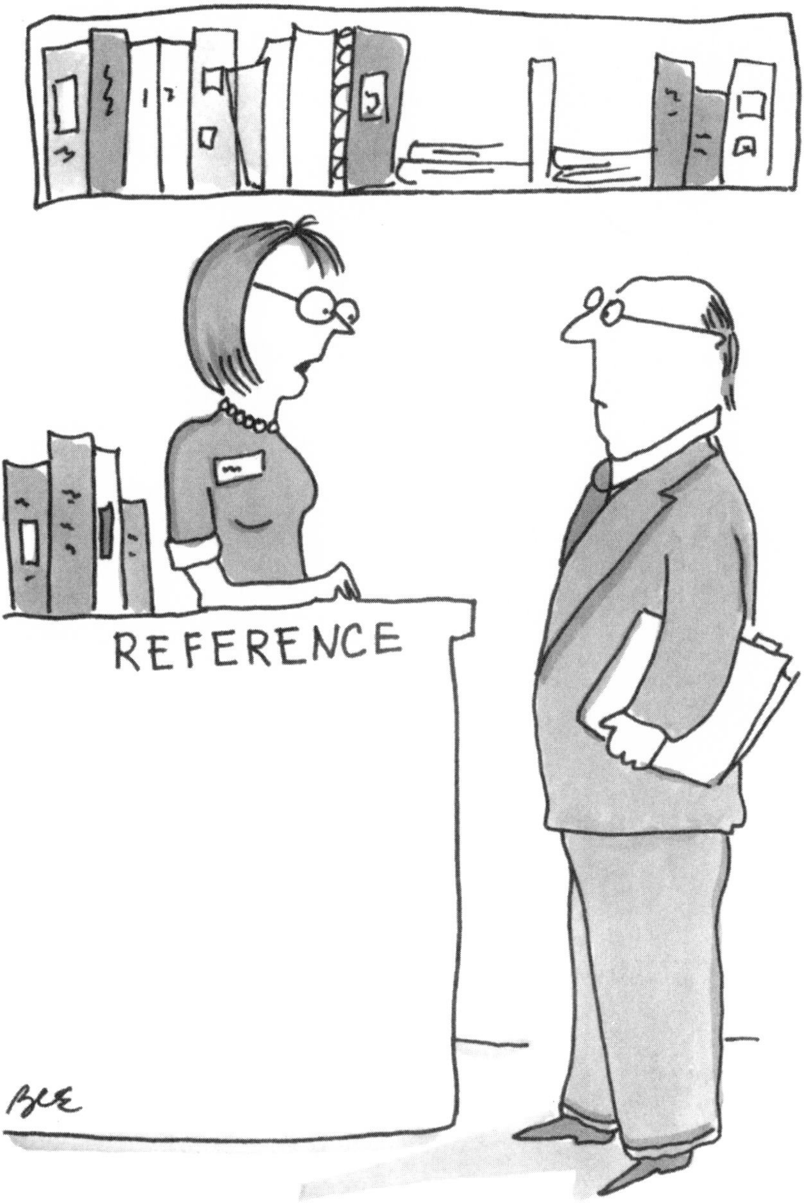
REFERENCE

"Sorry, sir. We don't conduct library searches for one's keys."

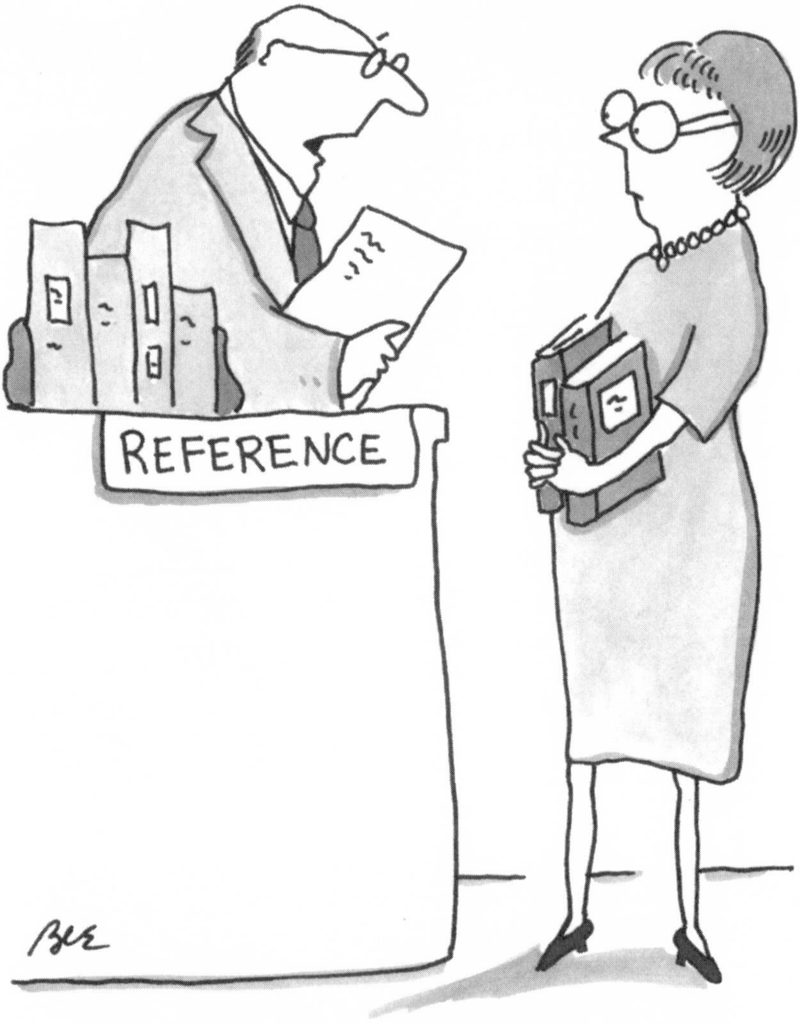
REFERENCE

"You want references for 'what I did on my summer vacation'? Are you sure you're not doing your child's homework?"

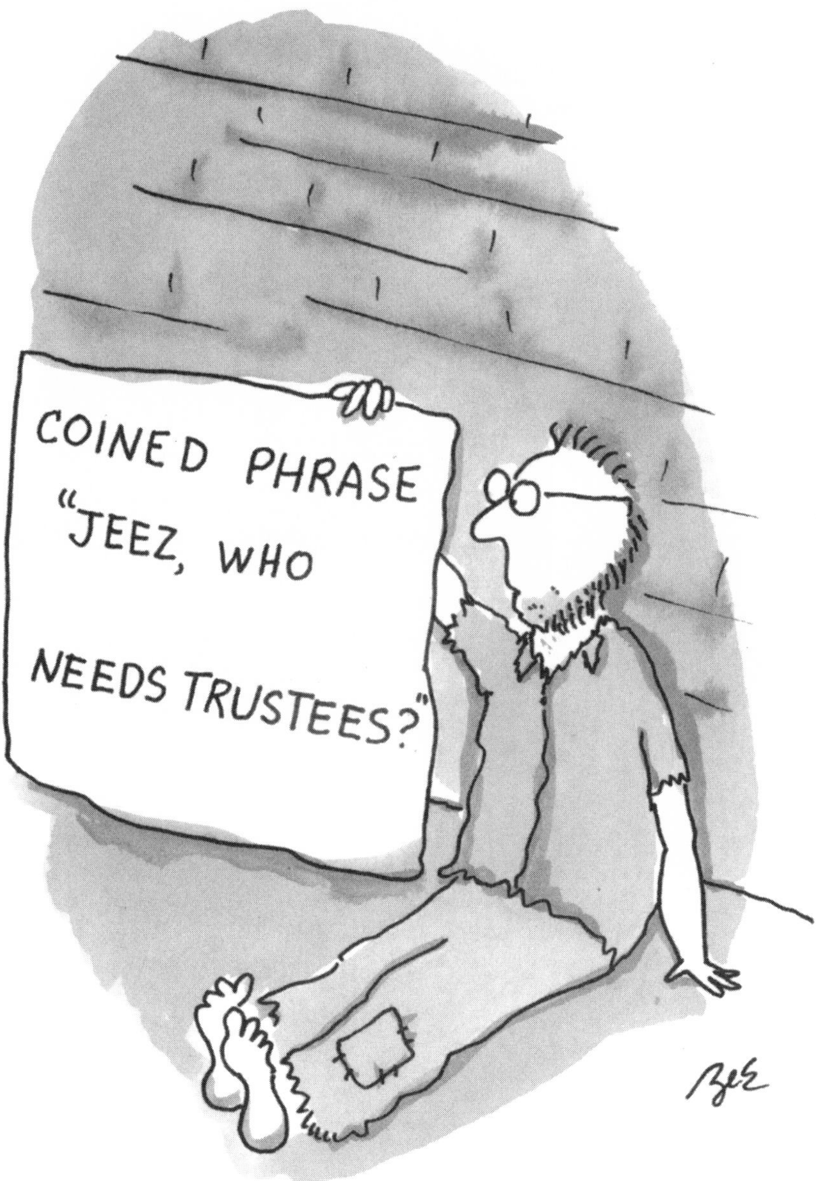
COINED PHRASE
"JEEZ, WHO
NEEDS TRUSTEES?"

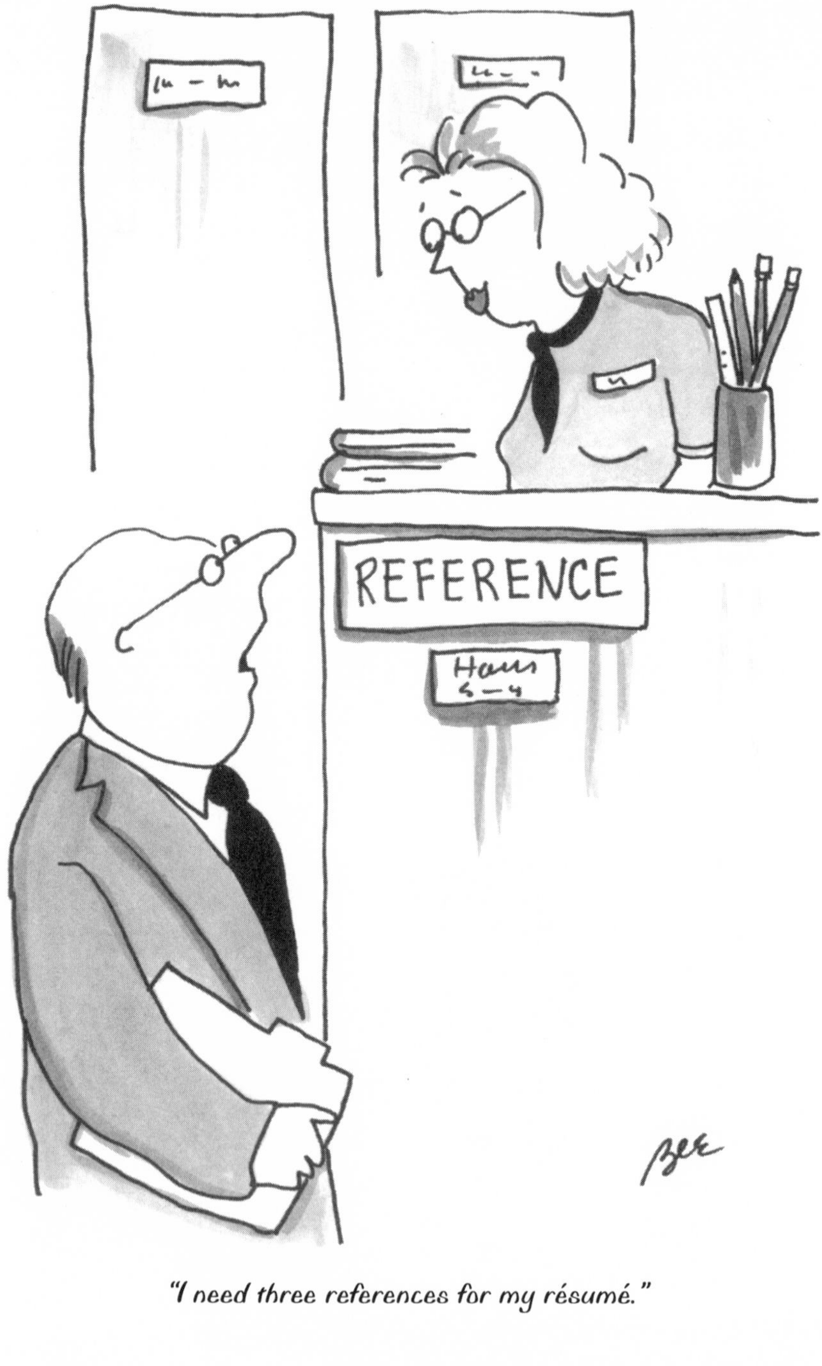
REFERENCE

"I need three references for my résumé."

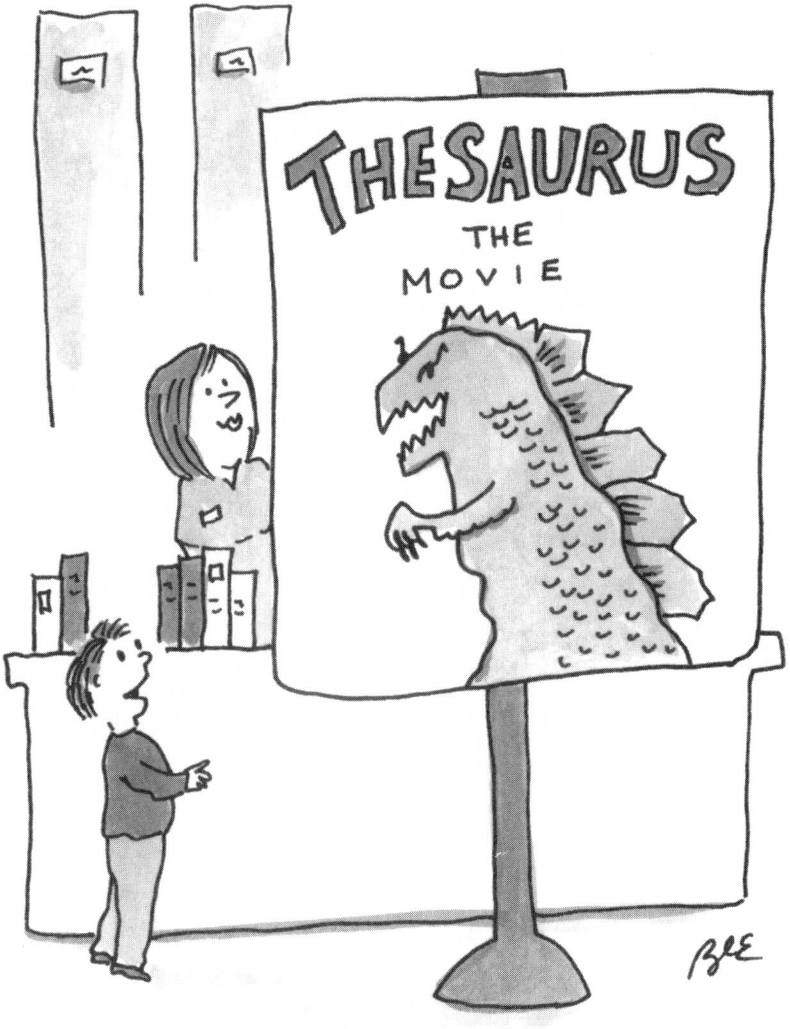
THESAURUS
THE
MOVIE

"Say, does that come in book form?"

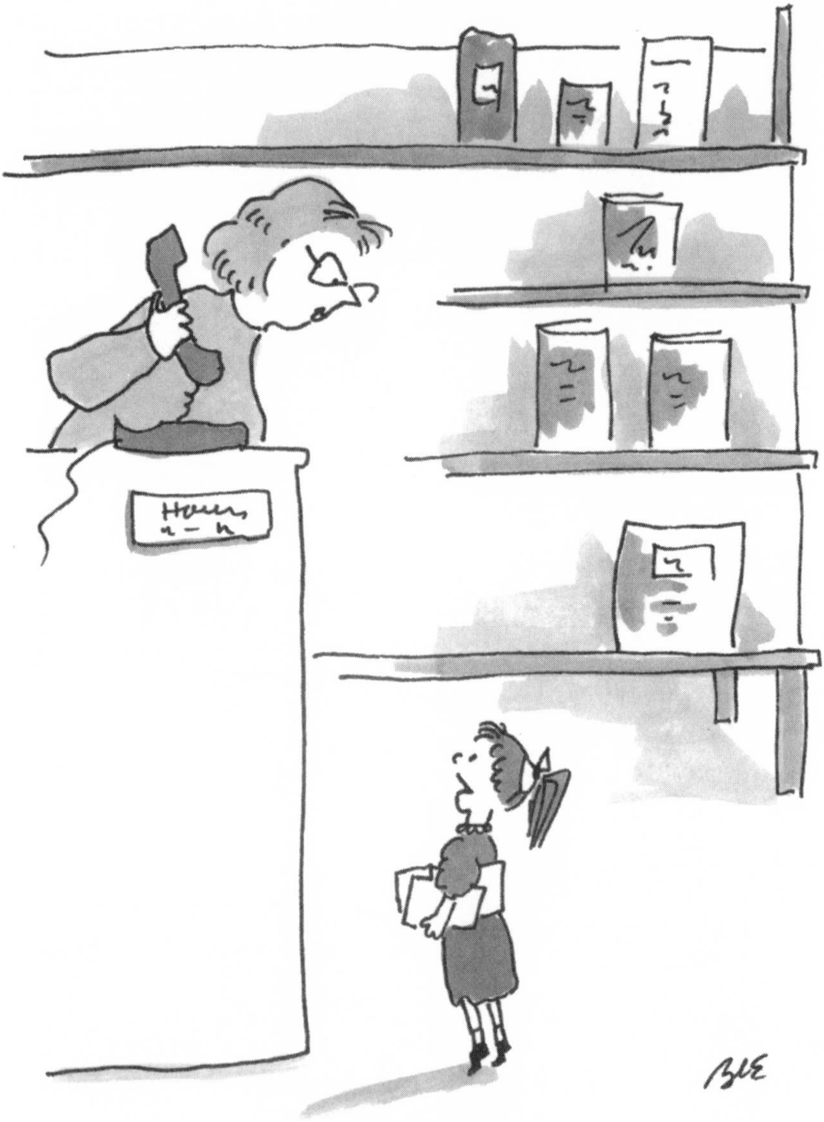

"Would you hold my calls?"

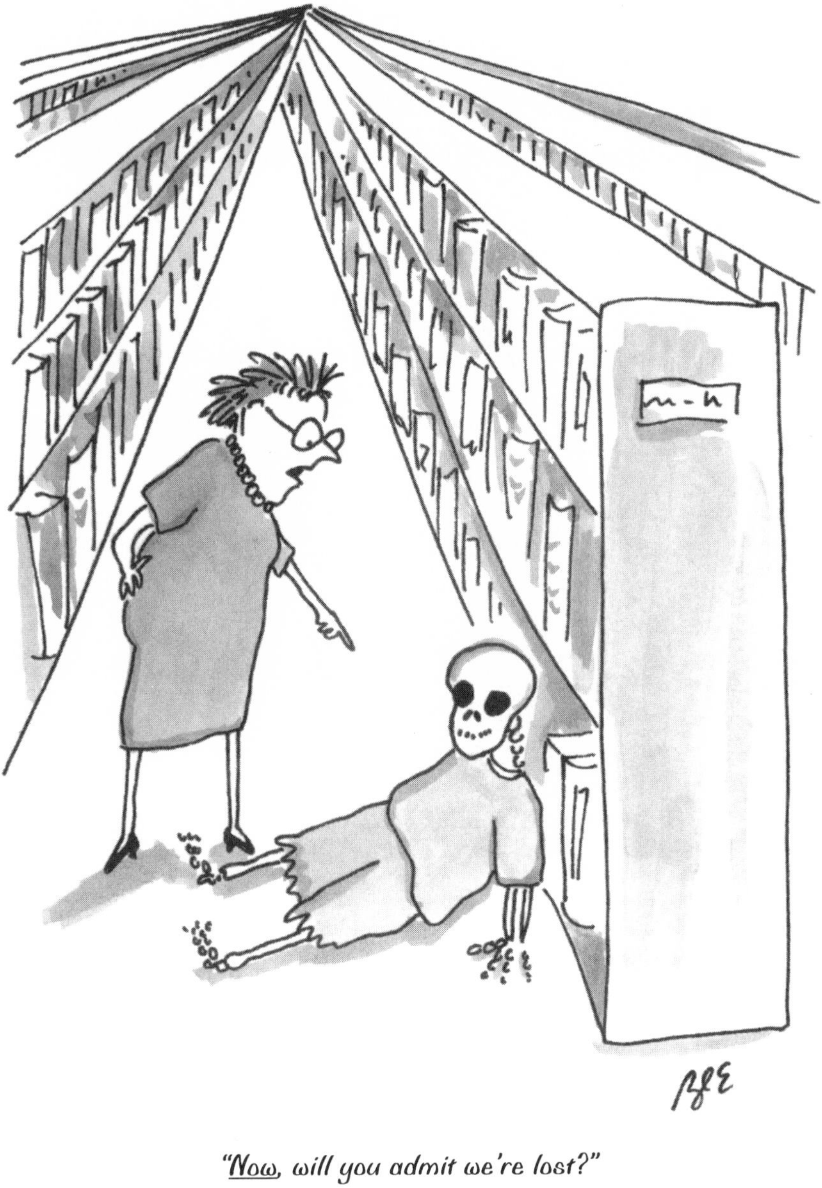

"Now, will you admit we're lost?"

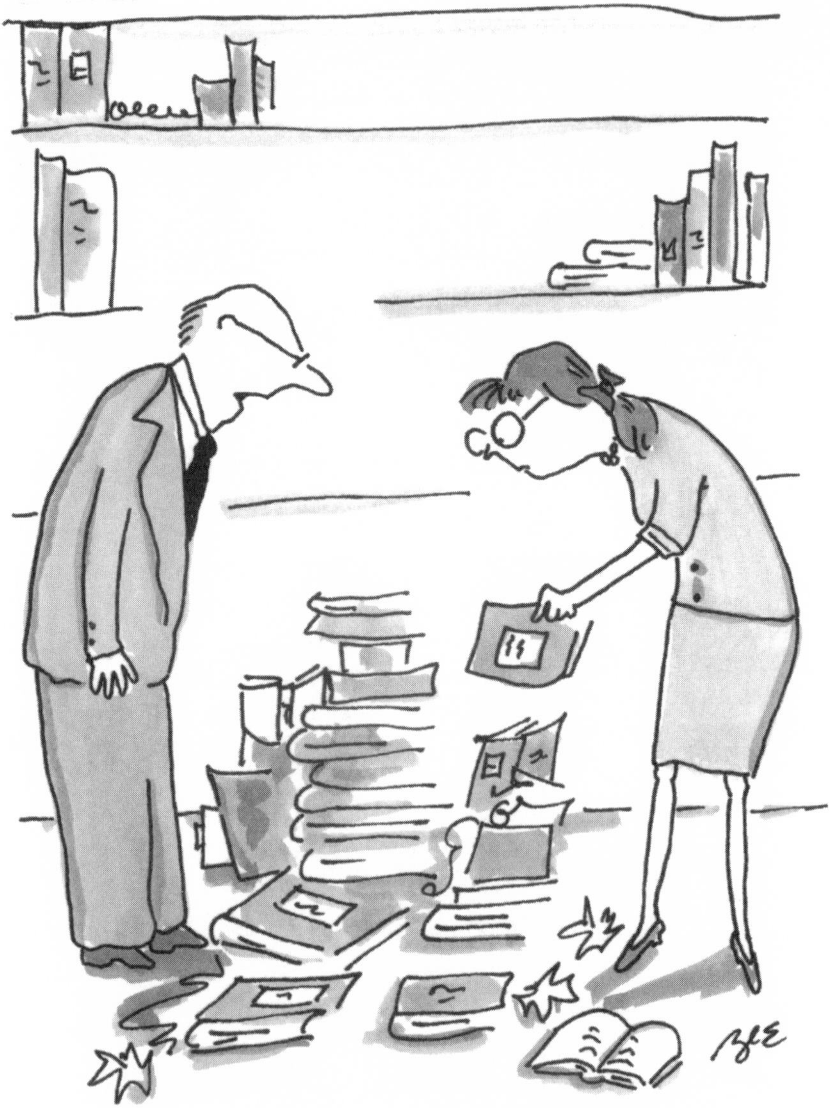

"Weed 'em and weep."

"Great news! I got a grant to learn how to write a grant."

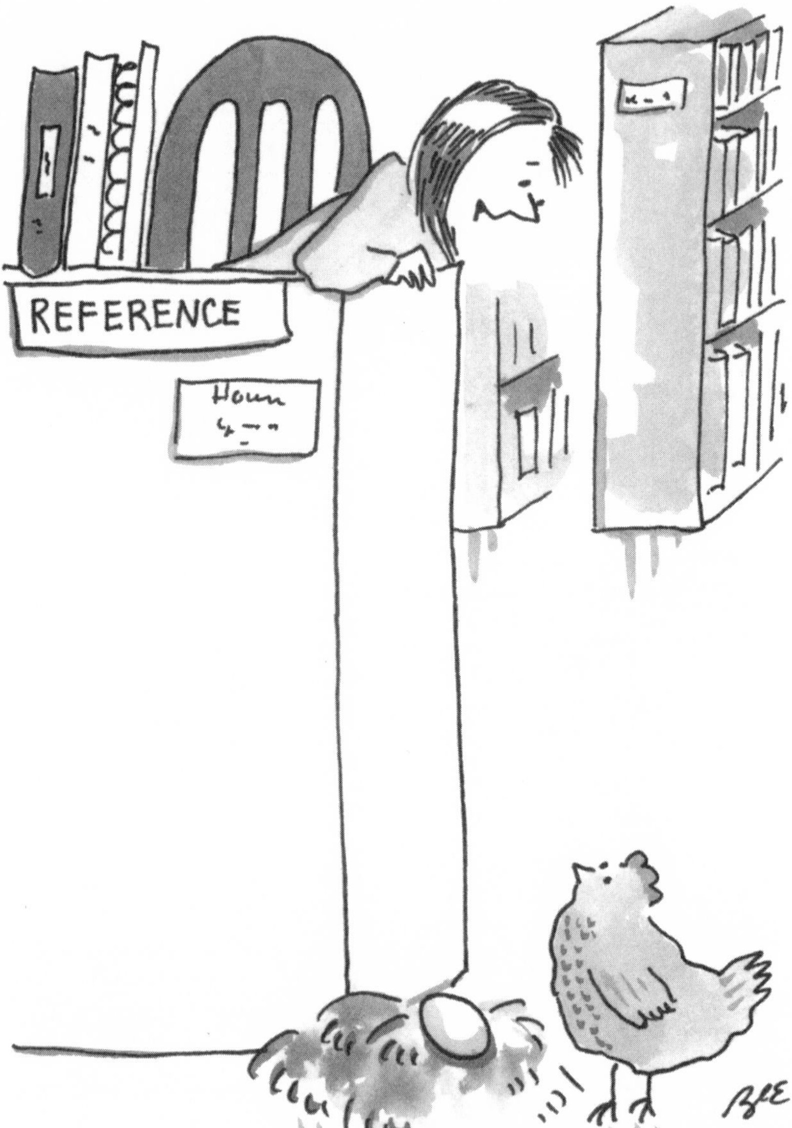
REFERENCE

"Who's first?"

"Twenty years ago I became a librarian.
Now, I don't know what the heck I am."

"Did the title have any other words besides 'the'?"

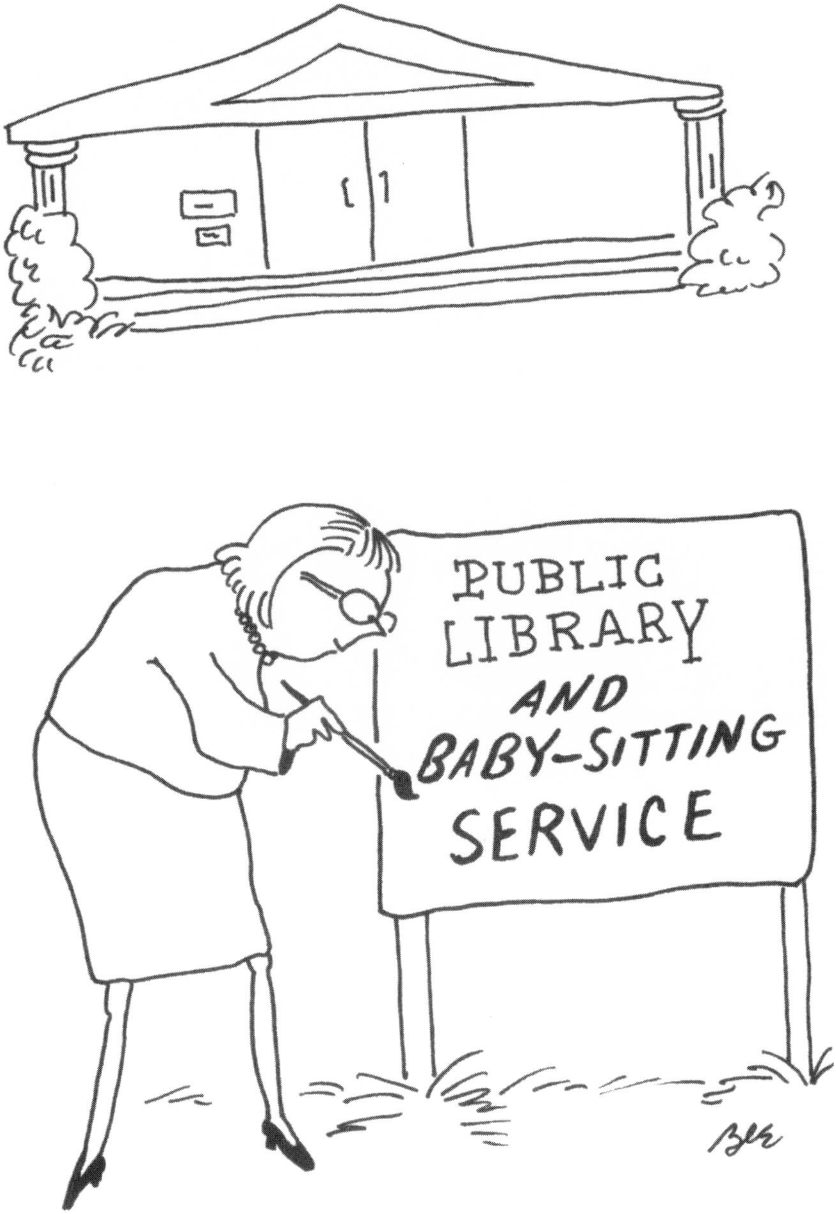
PUBLIC
LIBRARY
AND
BABY-SITTING
SERVICE

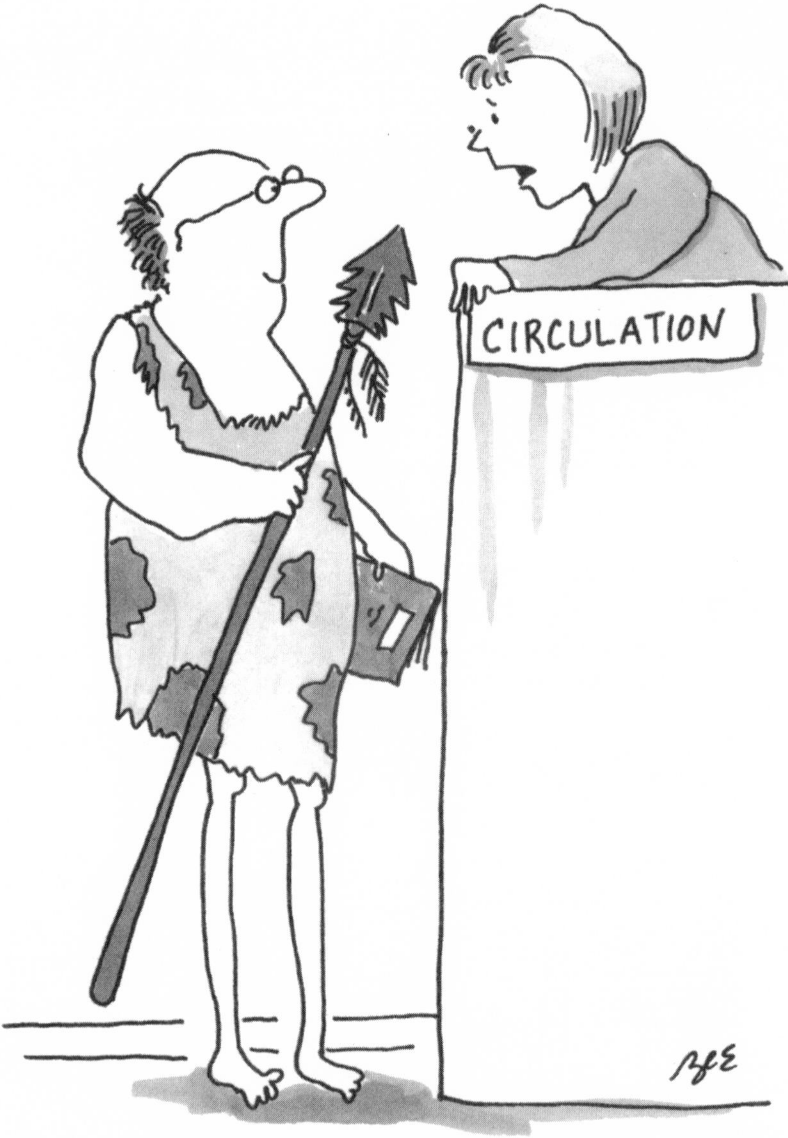
CIRCULATION

"No, you won't be charged for books you checked out in a previous life."

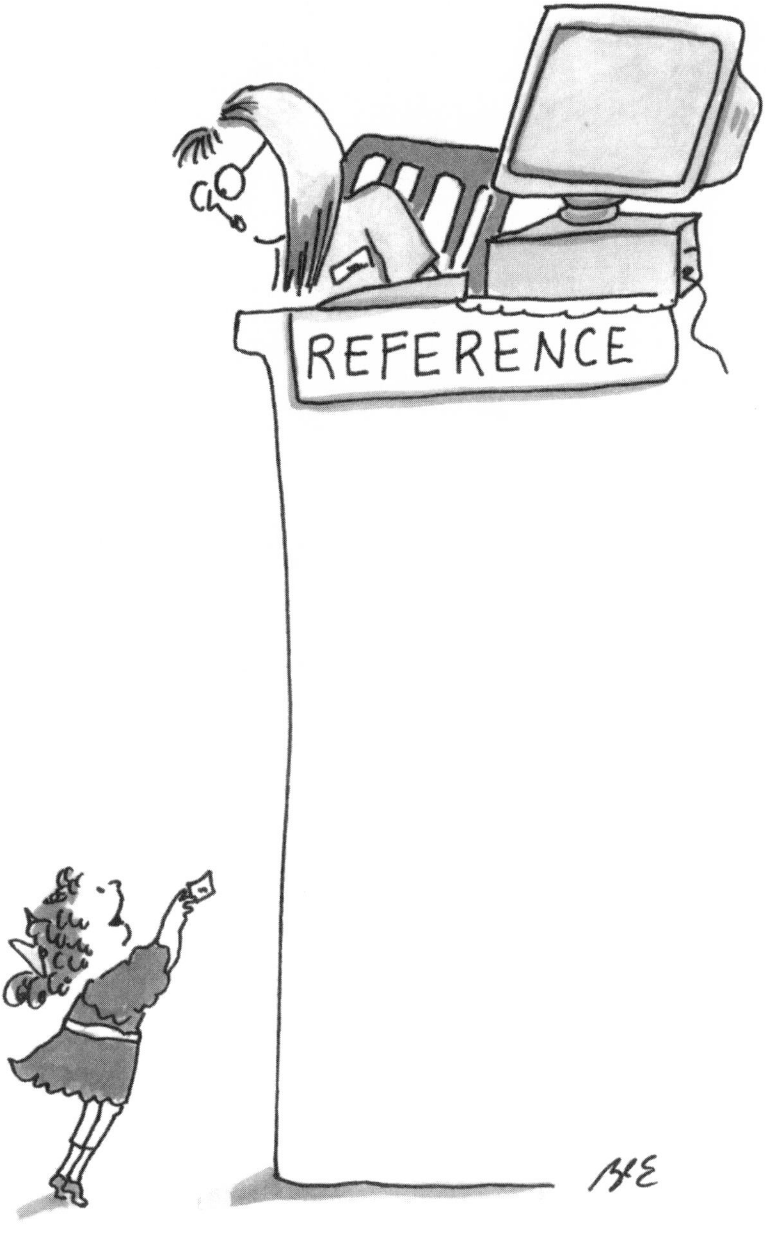
REFERENCE

"...and if you ever have any questions here's my card."

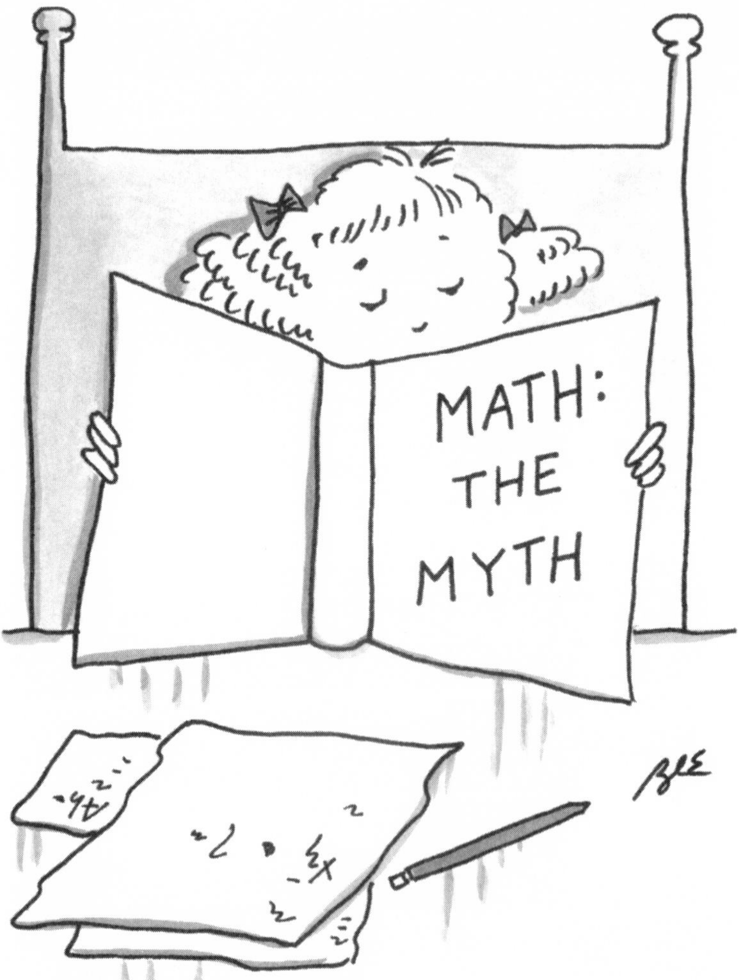
MATH:
THE
MYTH

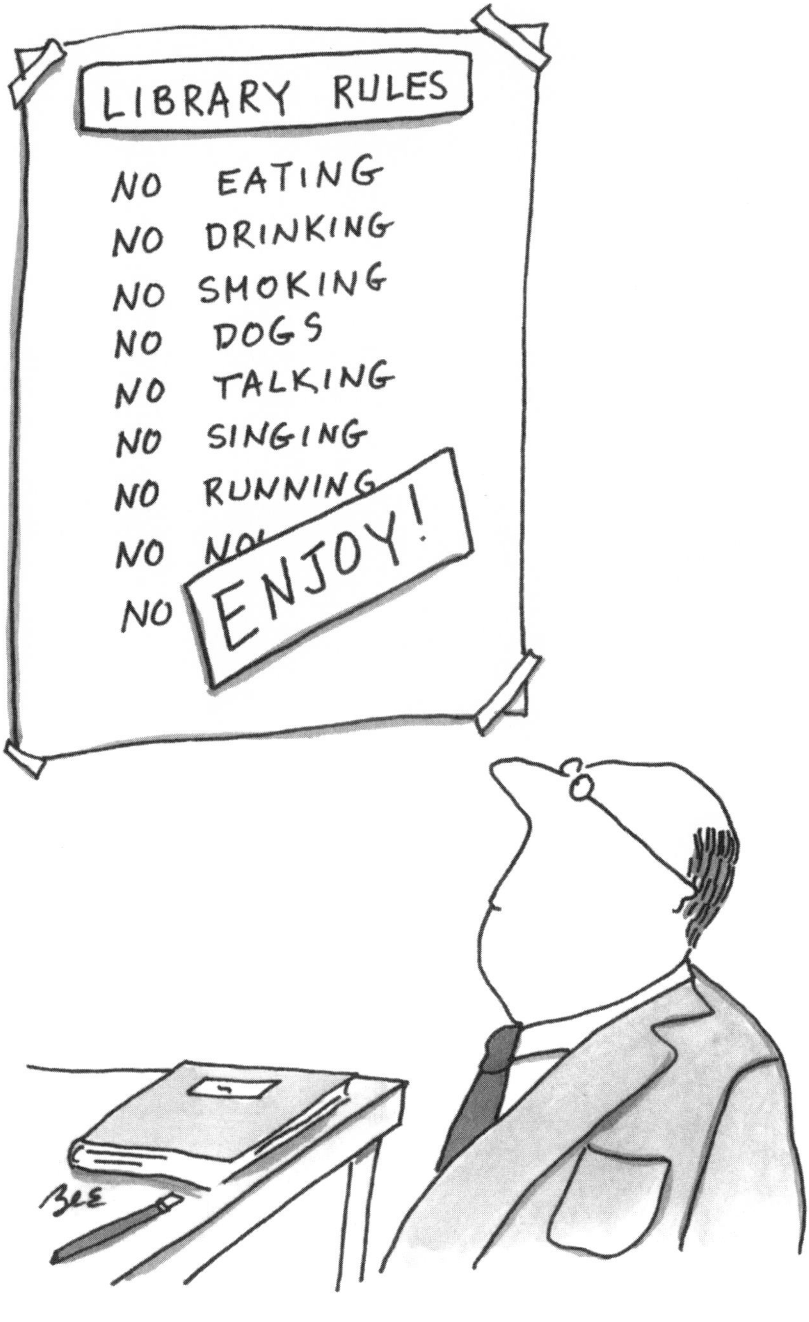
LIBRARY RULES
NO EATING
NO DRINKING
NO SMOKING
NO DOGS
NO TALKING
NO SINGING
NO RUNNING
NO
NO
ENJOY!

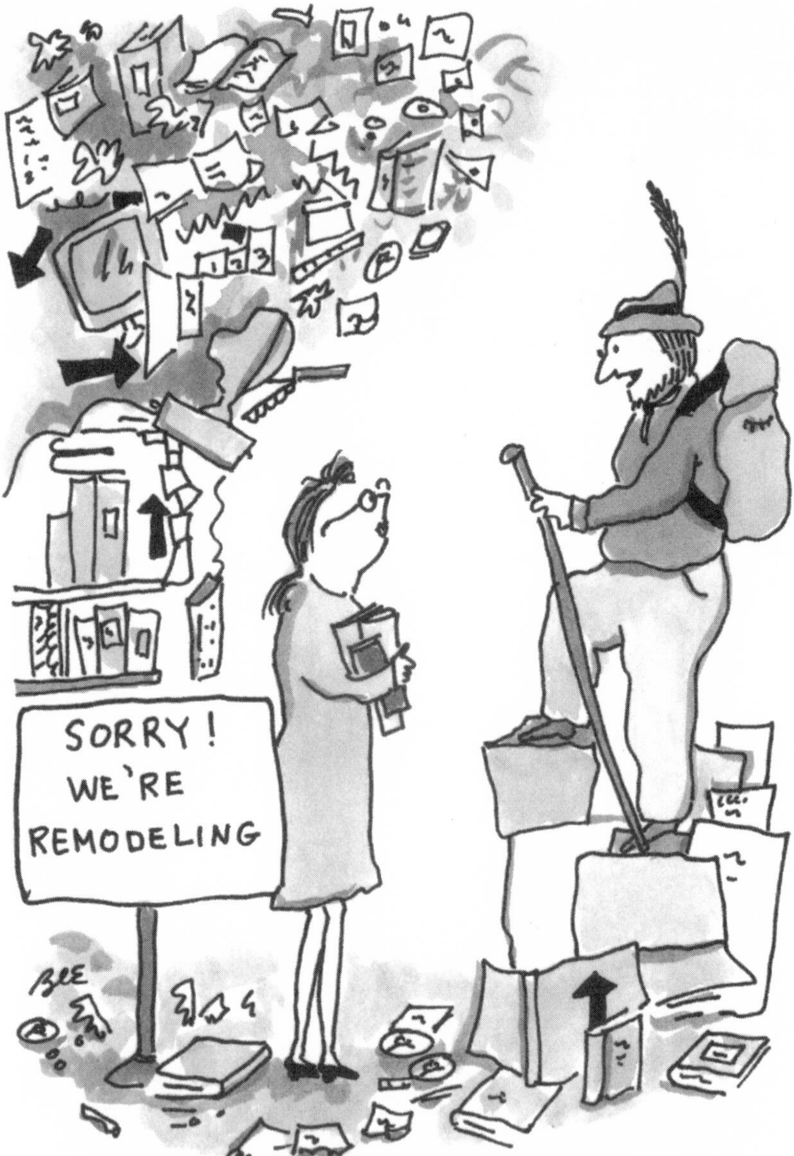
SORRY!
WE'RE
REMODELING
BEE

"I am Ignacio. I'll be your guide."

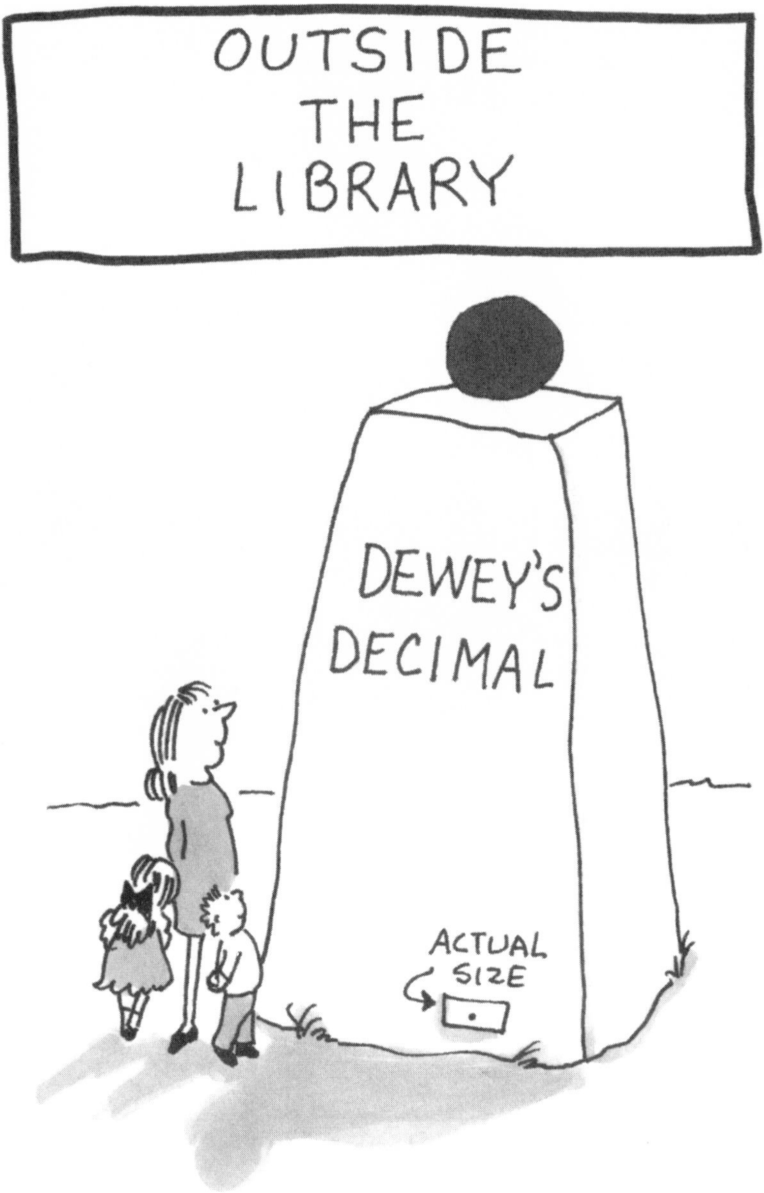
OUTSIDE THE LIBRARY
DEWEY'S DECIMAL
ACTUAL SIZE

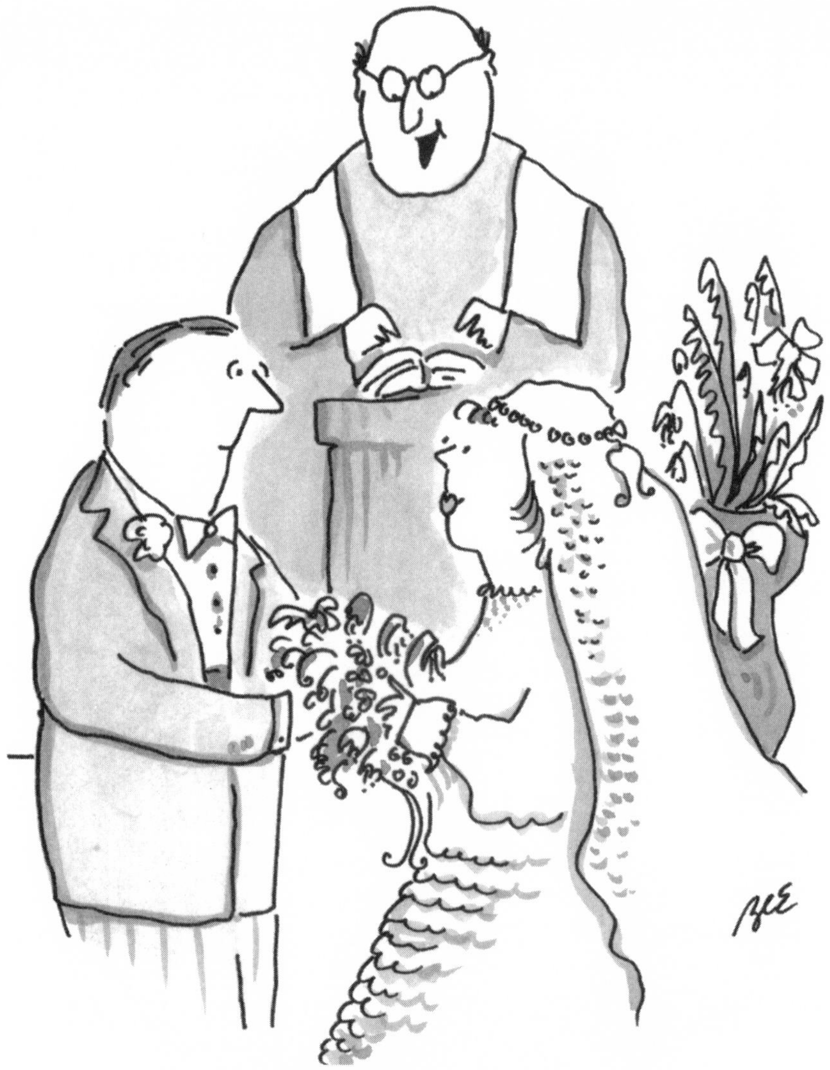

"And do you take Ted, so the library can keep its programmer, or do you really love the guy?"

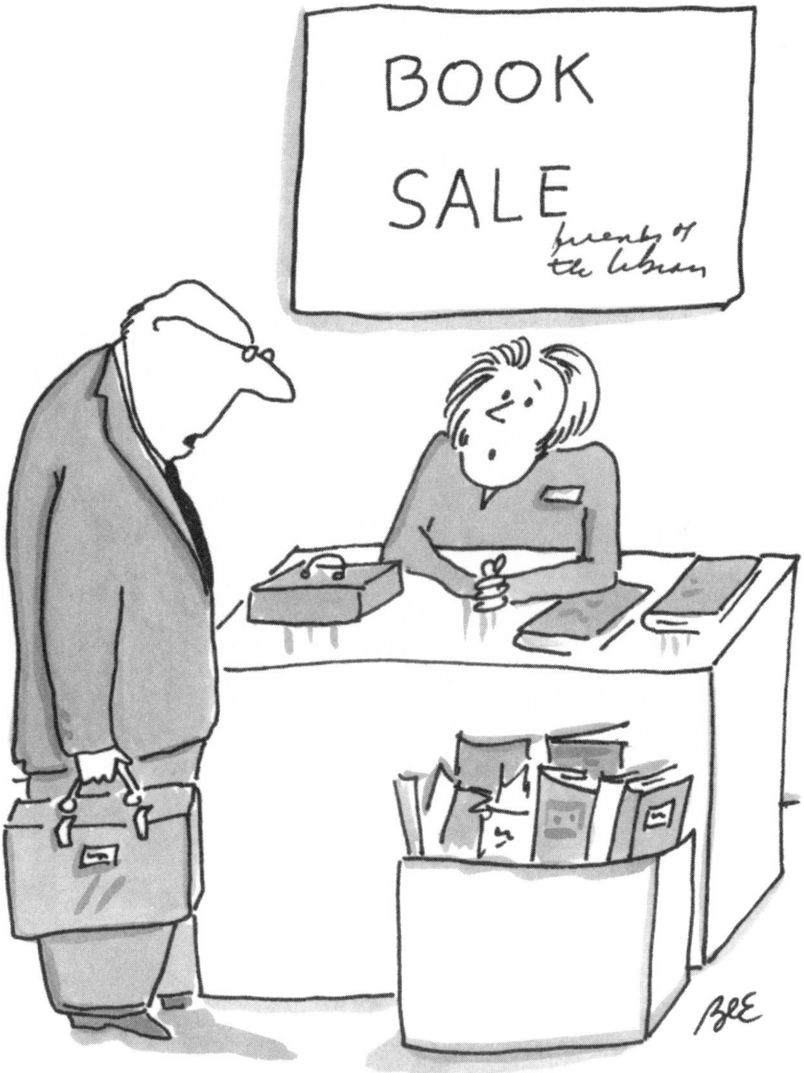
BOOK
SALE

"No, thank you. I have a book."

"You're a librarian? How did you become interested in knowledge?"

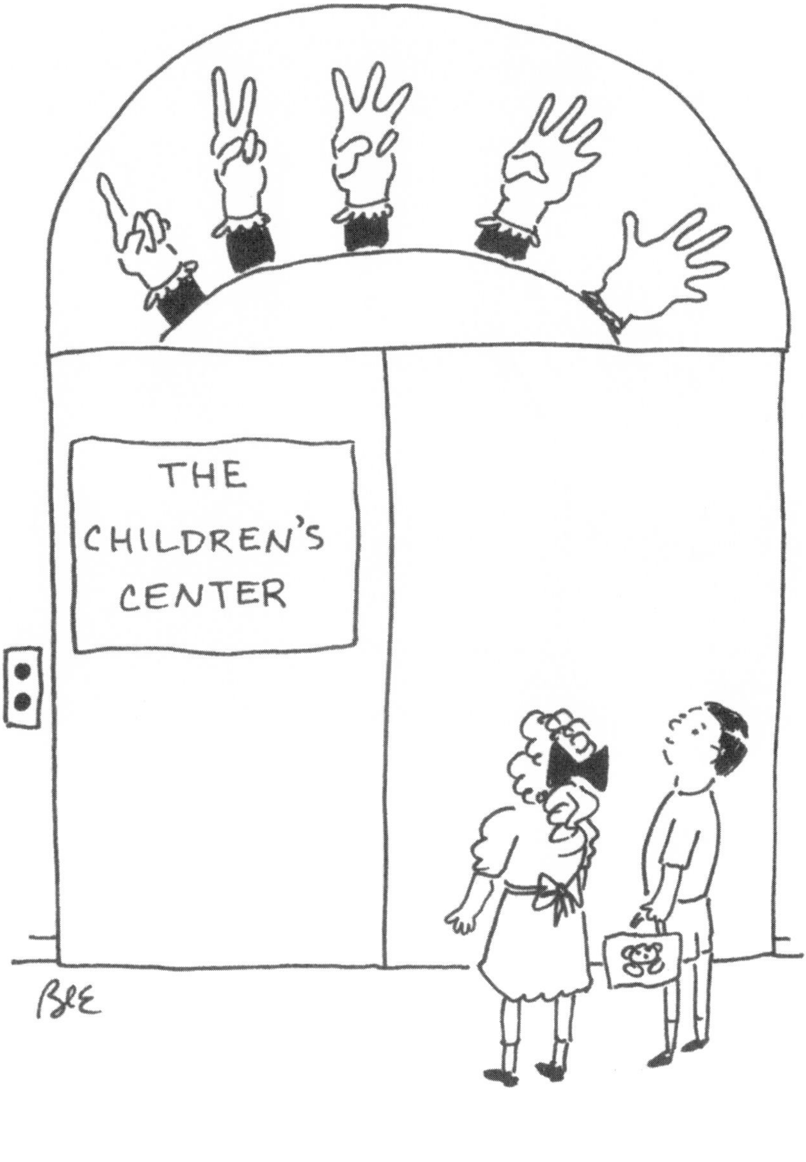
THE CHILDREN'S CENTER
BEE

"Your future as a librarian? You will enjoy ... oops, it's changing. You will go on a long ... oops, it's changing again."

"Wake up! You're the next interesting speaker."

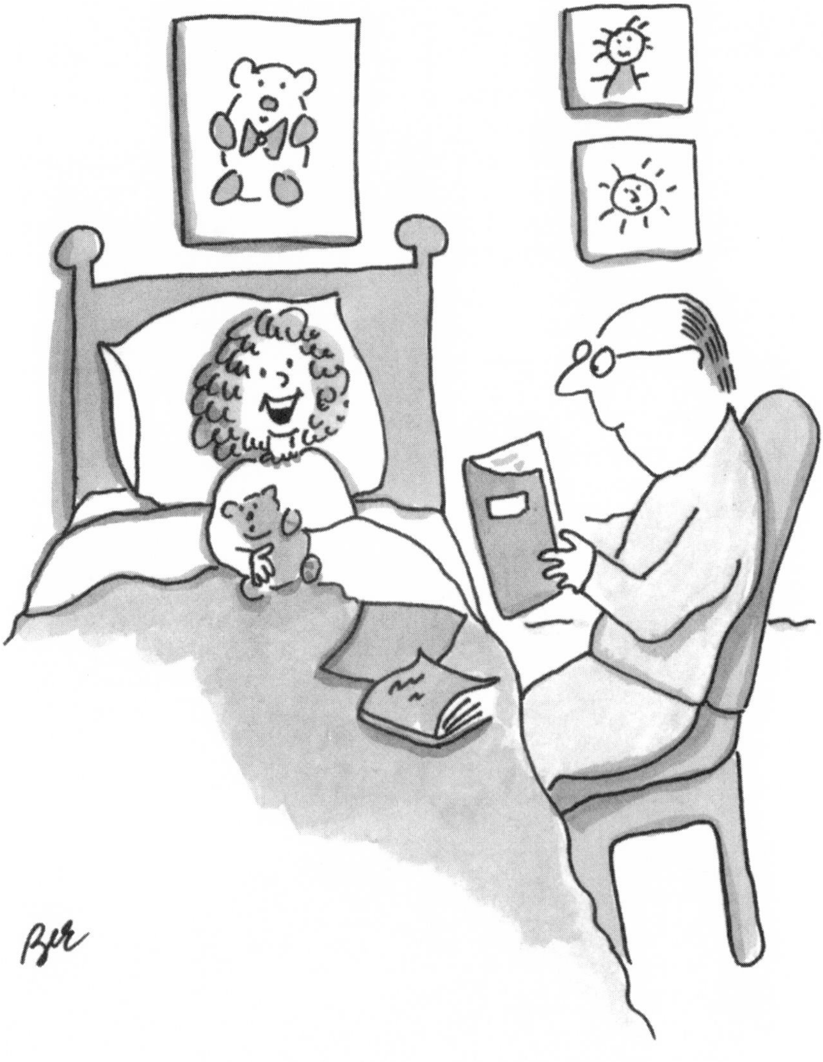
Bzr

"So, the prince had to deal with all the poor and disenfranchised? Was he a librarian?"

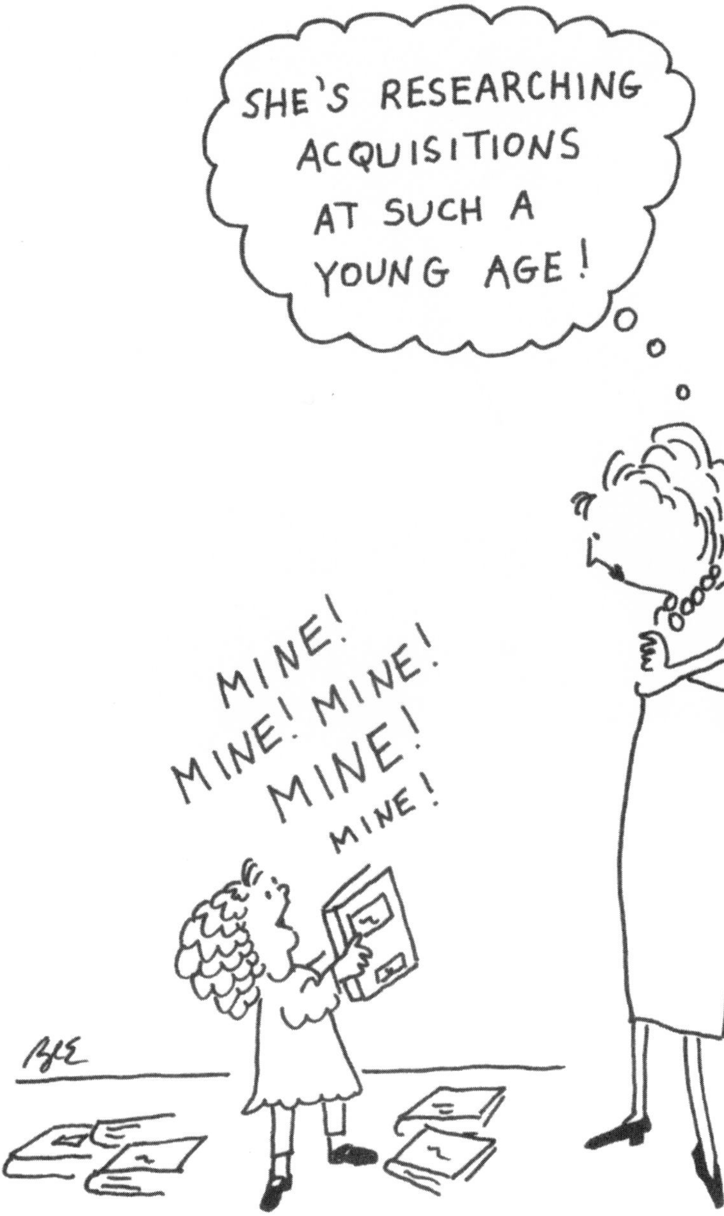
SHE'S RESEARCHING ACQUISITIONS AT SUCH A YOUNG AGE!
MINE!
MINE! MINE!
MINE!
MINE!

"How do you know you don't like the book?
You haven't even tasted it yet."

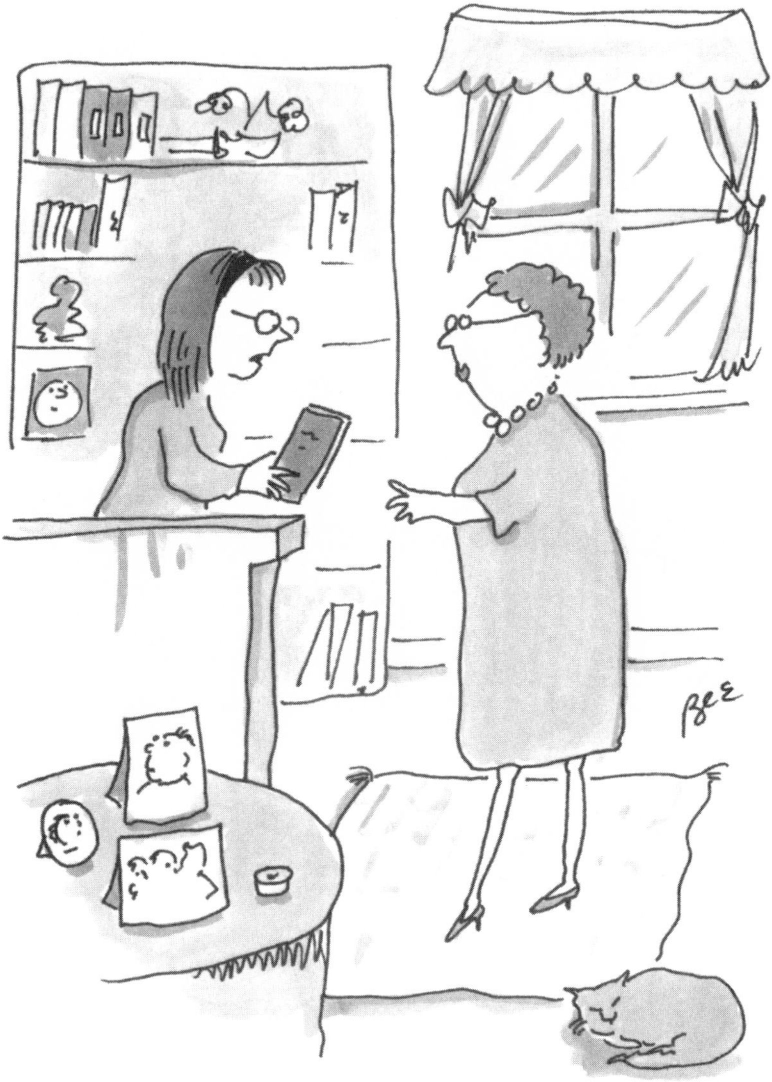
Bee

"This video of Billy's first day of school is due back in three weeks, Mom!"

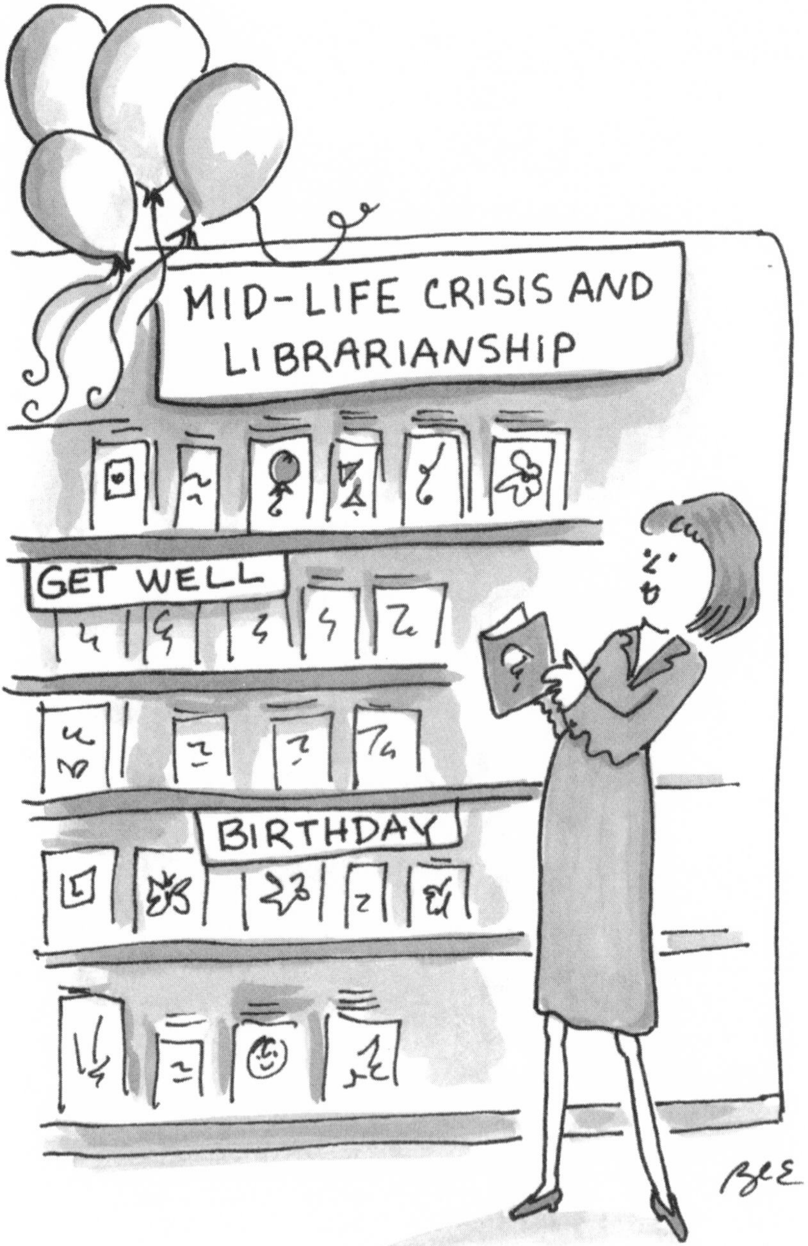
MID-LIFE CRISIS AND LIBRARIANSHIP
GET WELL
BIRTHDAY
BEE

"I'll get the newspaper. What's your password?"

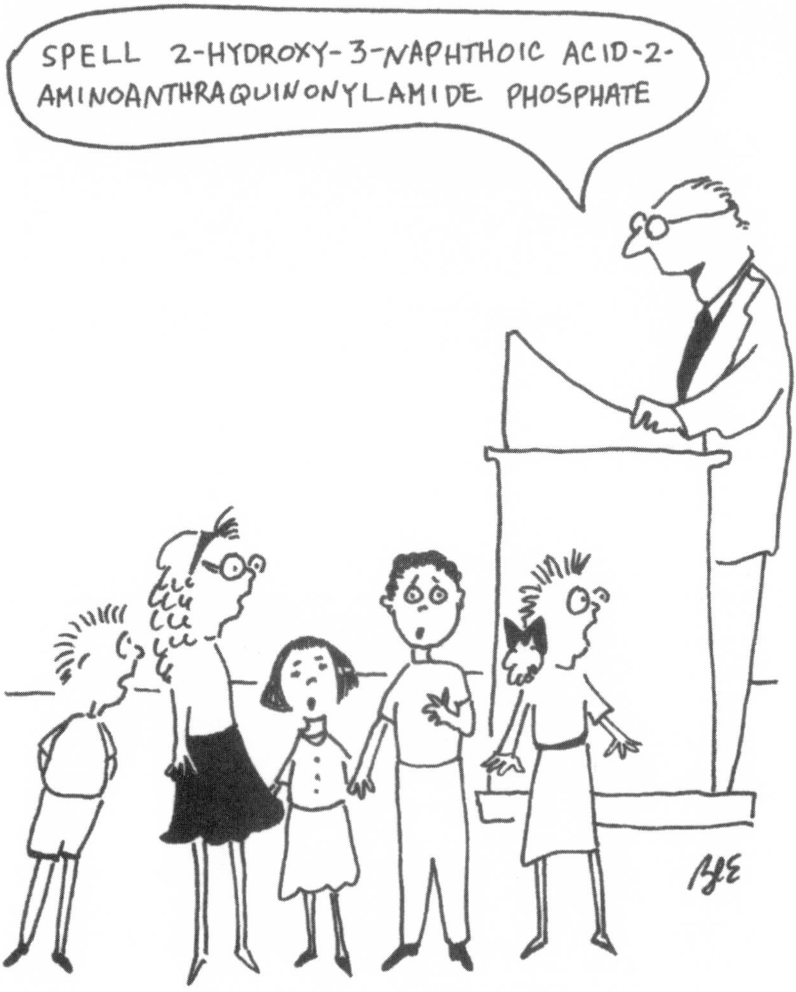
SPELL 2-HYDROXY-3-NAPHTHOIC ACID-2-AMINOANTHRAQUINONYLAMIDE PHOSPHATE

KILLER BEES

"There will be a brief question and
answer period following the lecture, Mom."

"All day long it's 'help,' 'search,' 'help,' 'search.' Know what I mean?"

"Gearing up for another day at the reference desk, dear?"

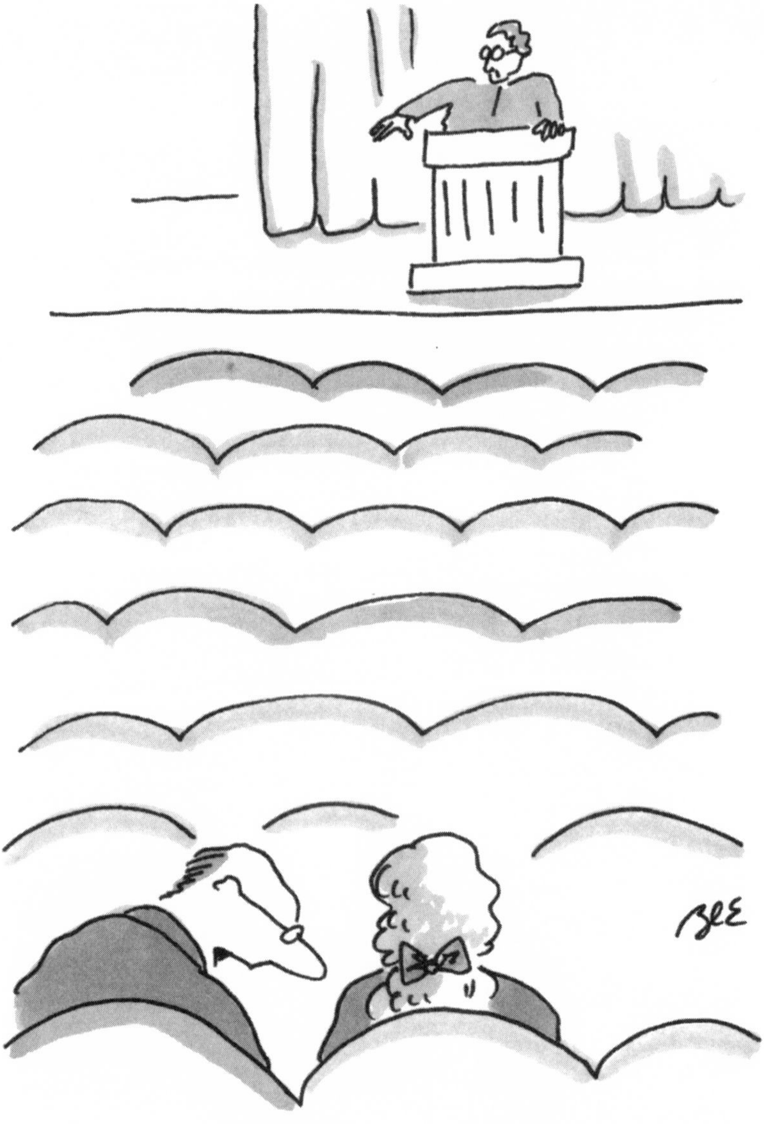
BEE

"It may be the word of God, but has he published anything?"

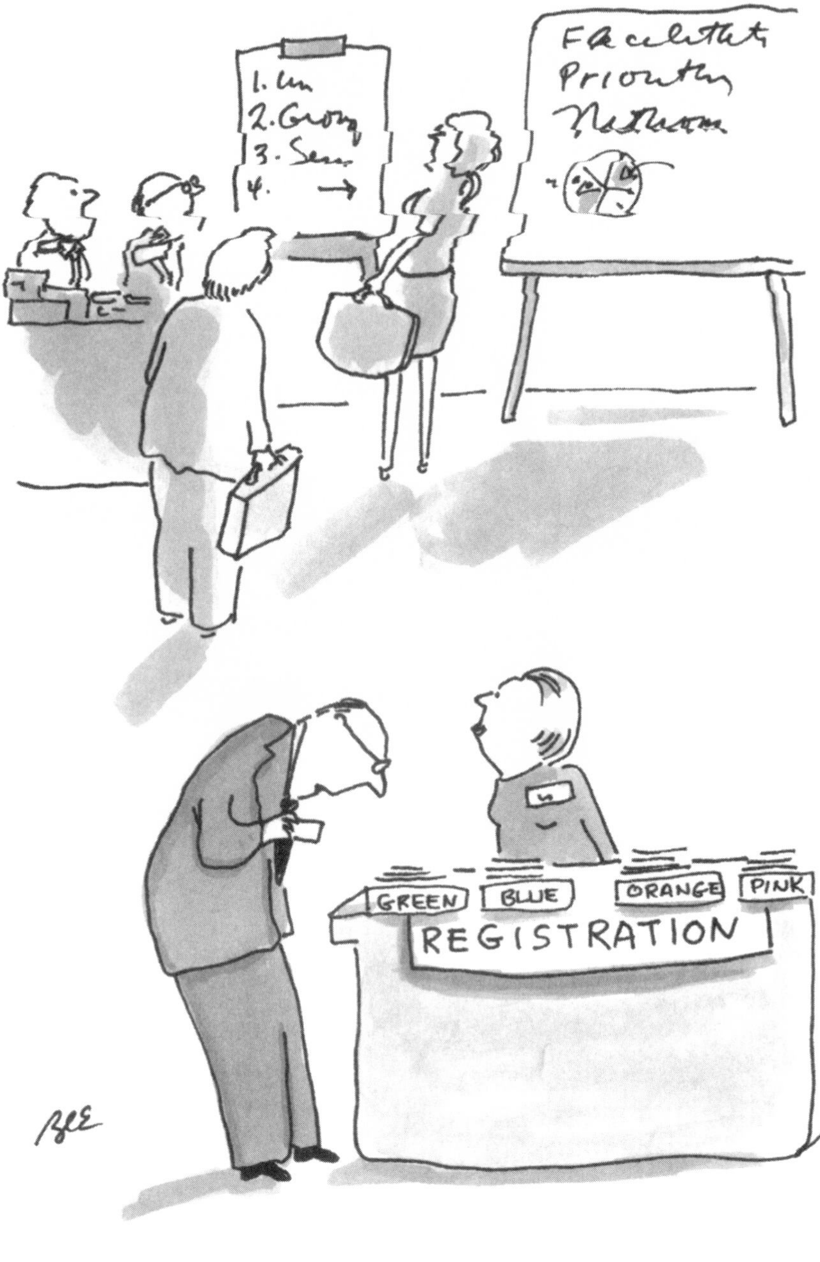
GREEN
BLUE
ORANGE
PINK
REGISTRATION

"Pardon me, but I can't be in the orange group. I'm a 'winter'."

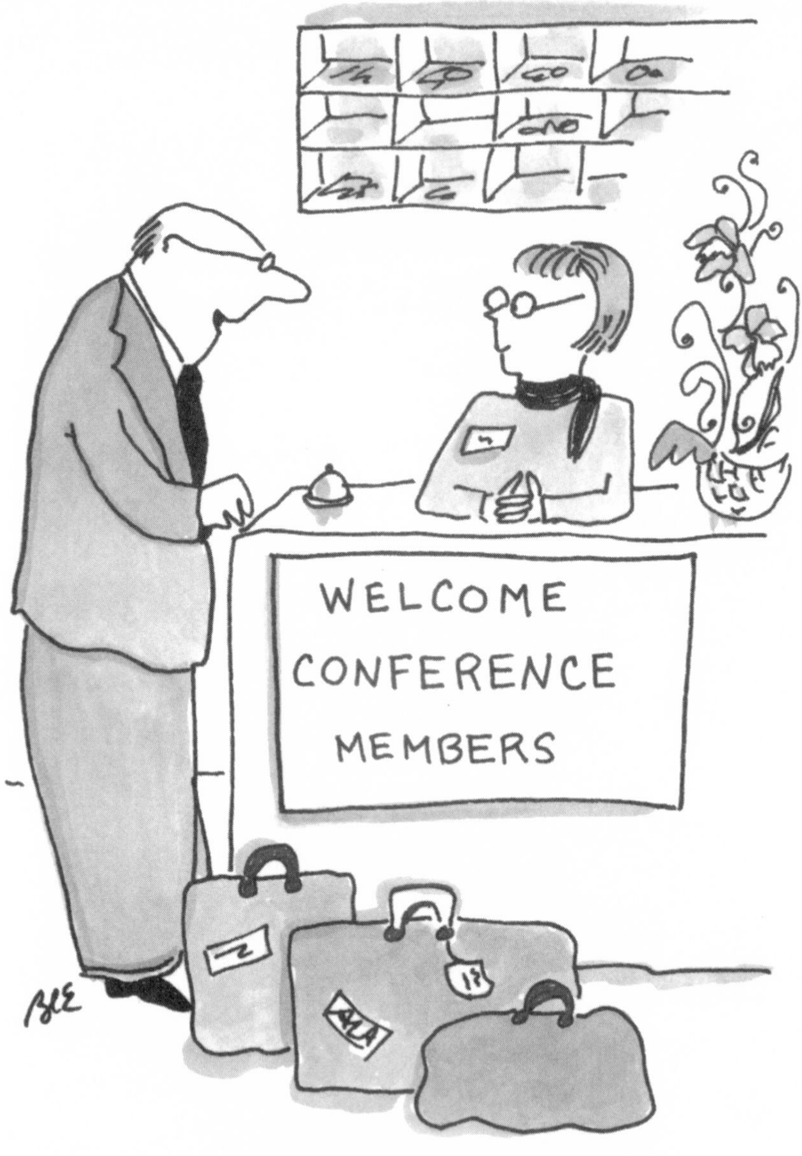
WELCOME
CONFERENCE
MEMBERS

"I'm only staying until I'm recognized."

"My mom fights more battles than your mom. Mine's a librarian."

"All you missed was 'the definition according to Webster's'."

"First, as an ice breaker … how many of you have tattoos?"

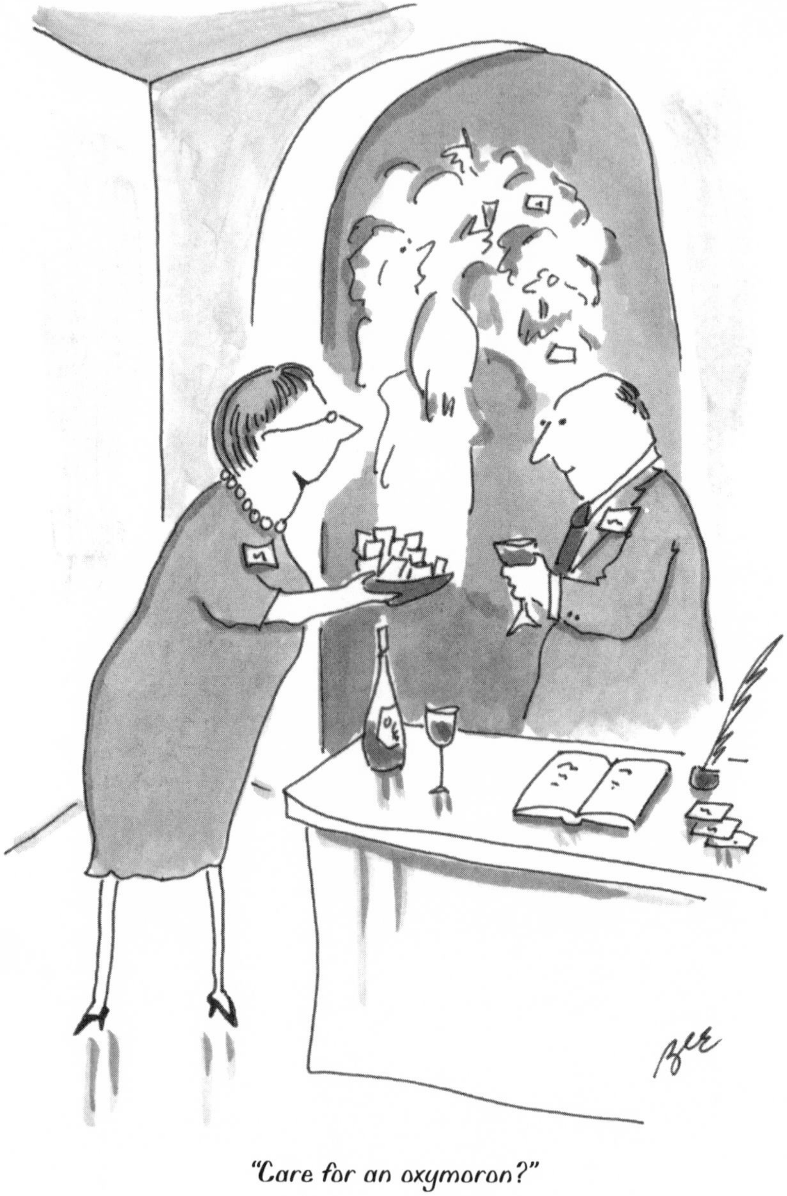
Zee

"Care for an oxymoron?"

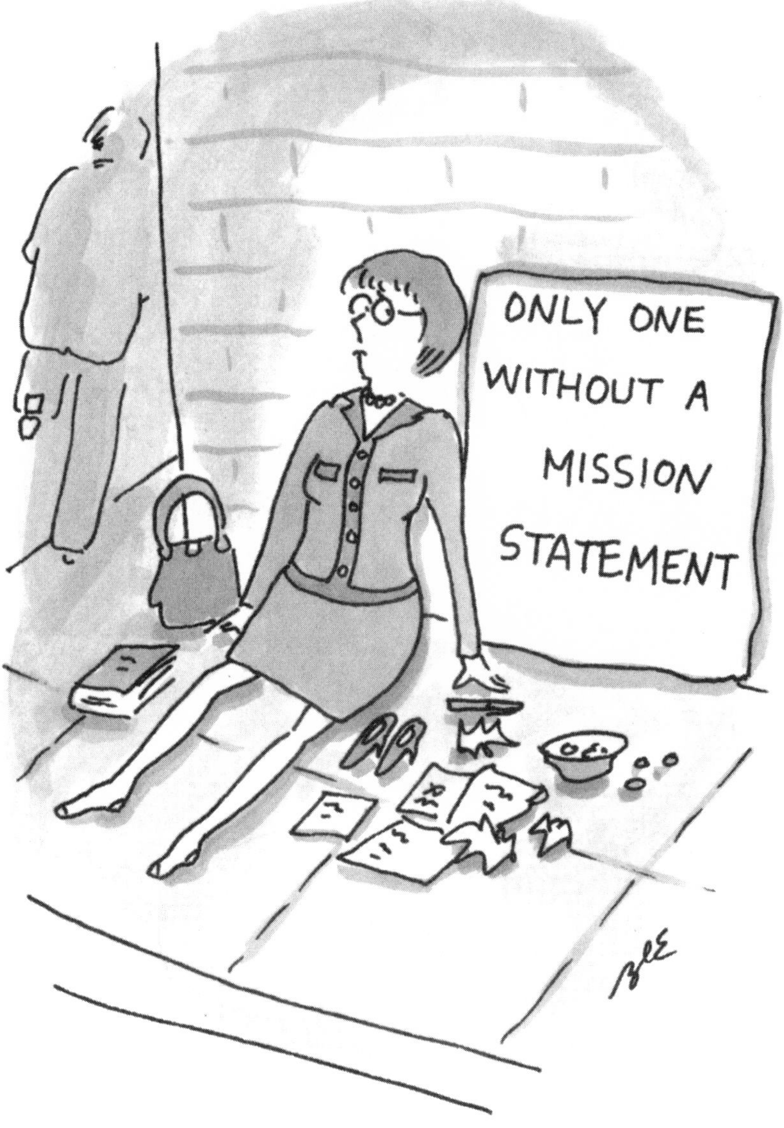
ONLY ONE WITHOUT A MISSION STATEMENT

"*I'm a librarian, not a liberian!*"

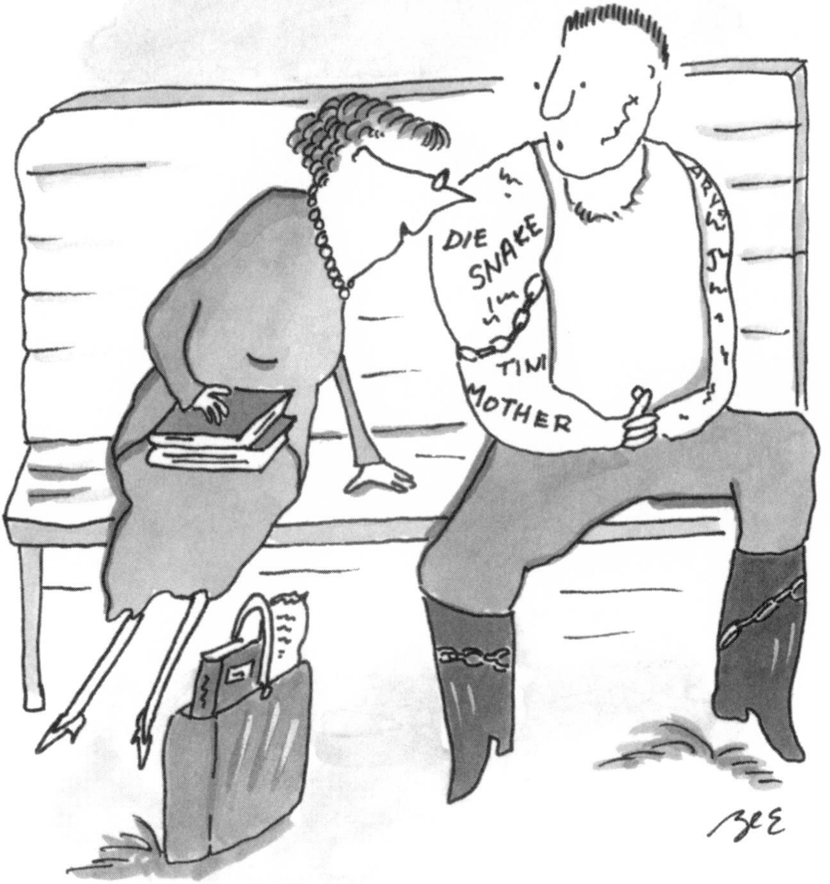
DIE
SNAKE
TINI
MOTHER

"I have a love of words, too."

TECHNOLOGY

I
SURVIVED
THE
INFORMATION
AGE

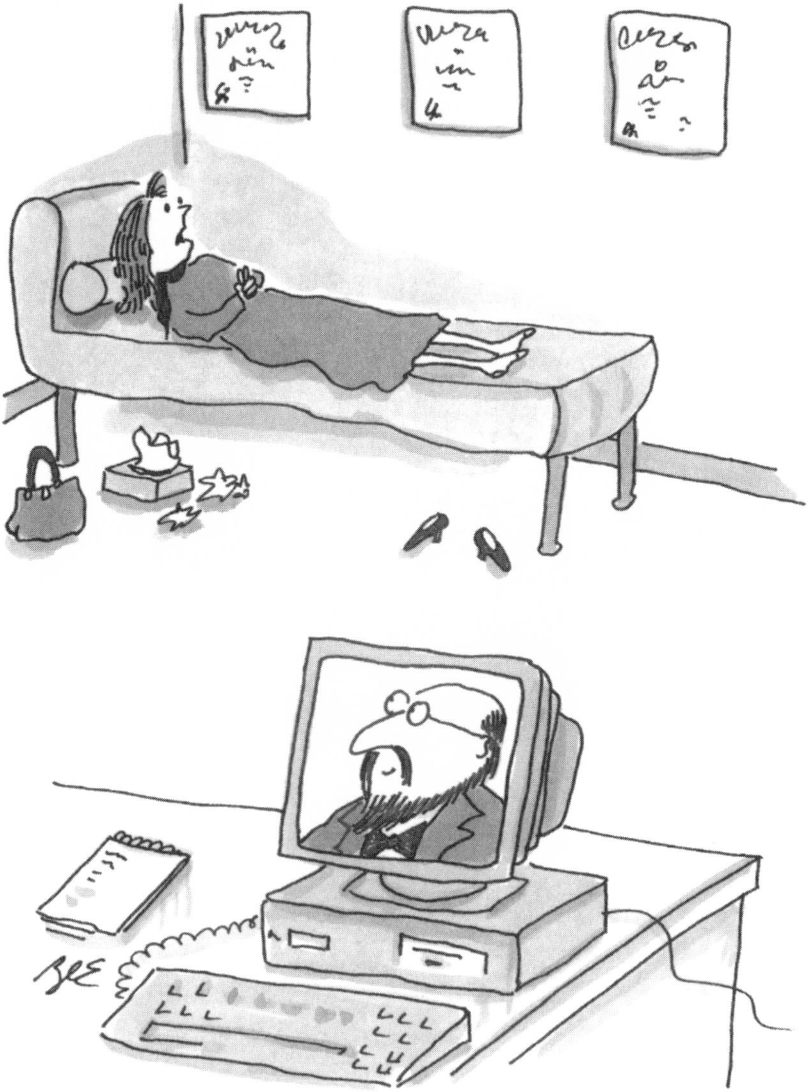

"I'm worried I'll be replaced by a computer."

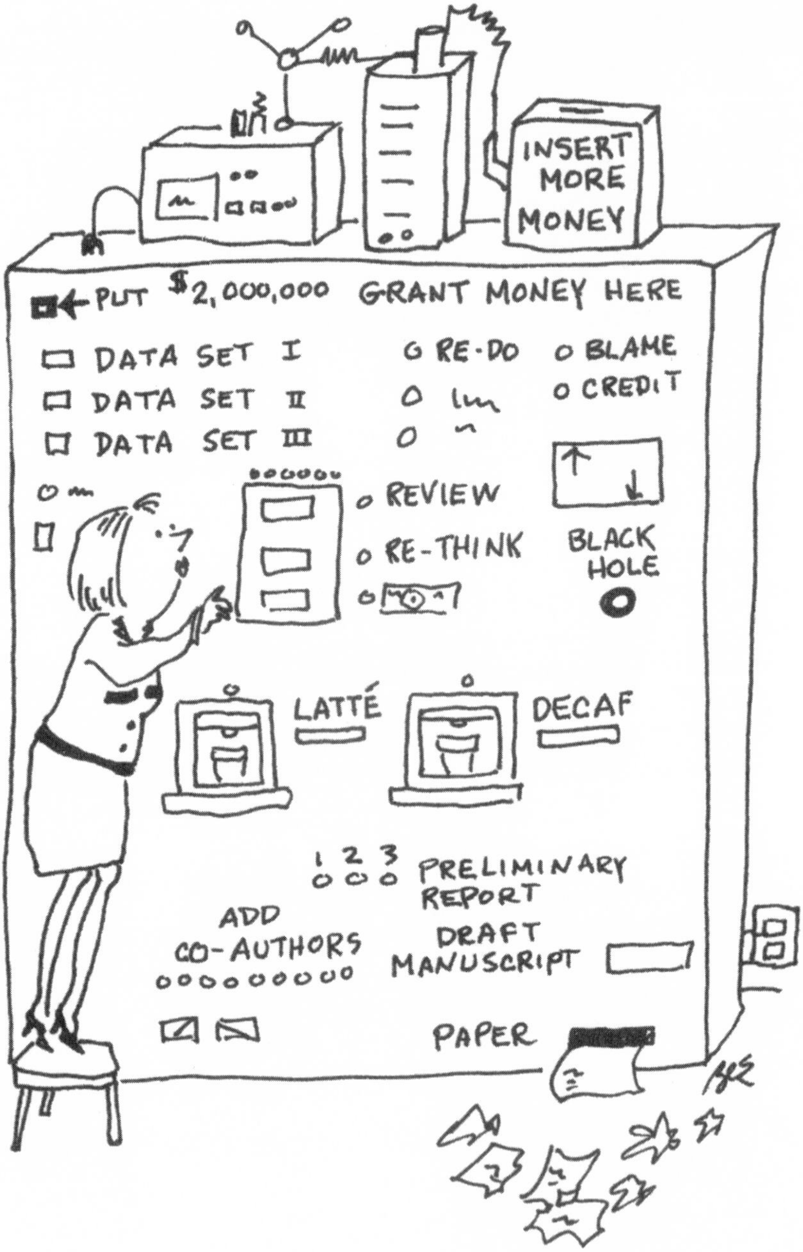
INSERT MORE MONEY
PUT $2,000,000 GRANT MONEY HERE
DATA SET I
DATA SET II
DATA SET III
RE-DO
BLAME
CREDIT
REVIEW
RE-THINK
BLACK HOLE
LATTÉ
DECAF
1 2 3
PRELIMINARY REPORT
ADD CO-AUTHORS
DRAFT MANUSCRIPT
PAPER

"You're due in three weeks."

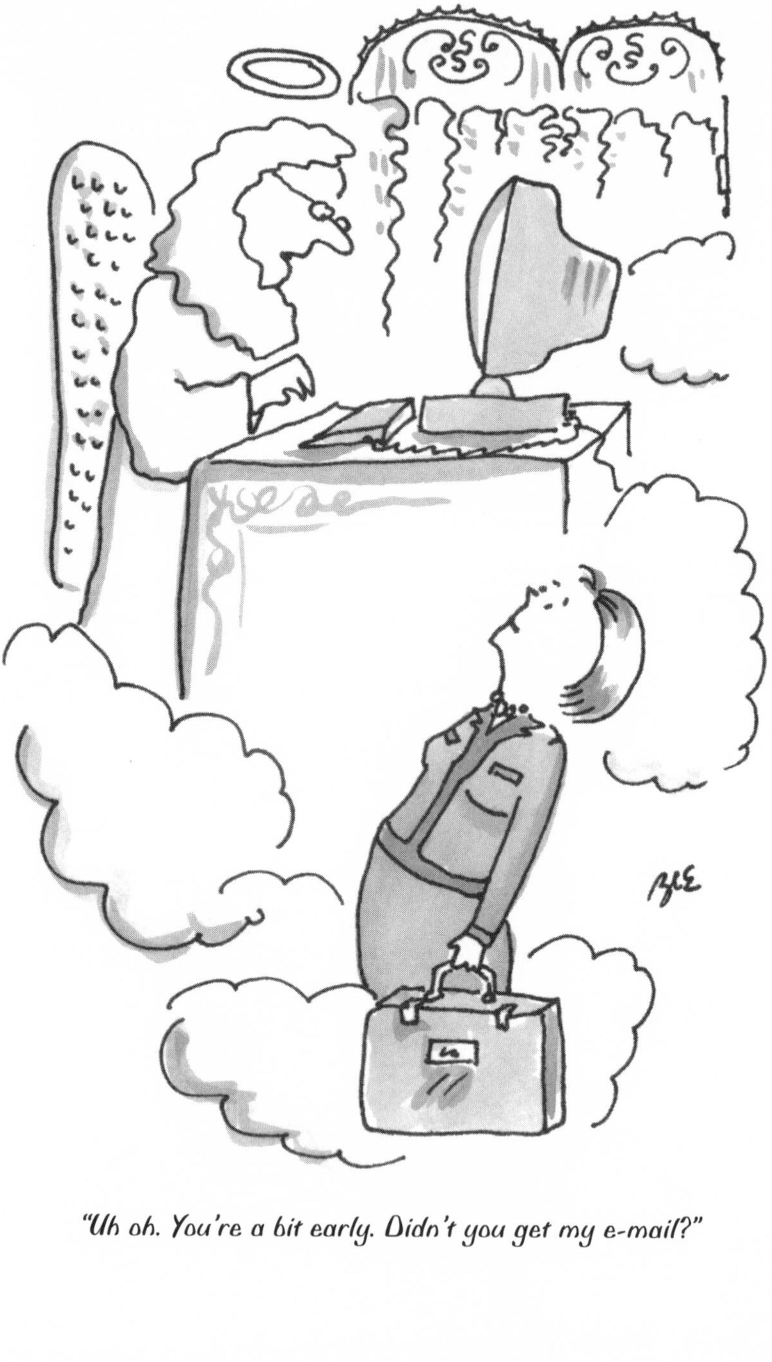
BE

"Uh oh. You're a bit early. Didn't you get my e-mail?"

"I'm faxing you something. What's your new area code?"

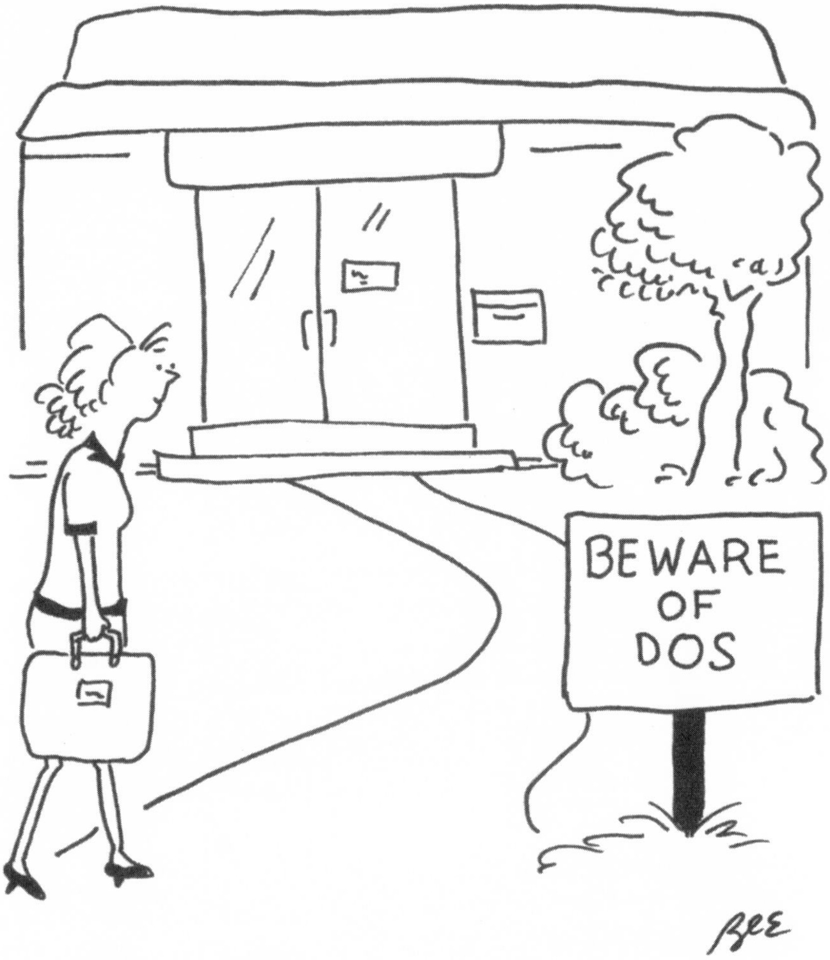
BEWARE
OF
DOS
BEE

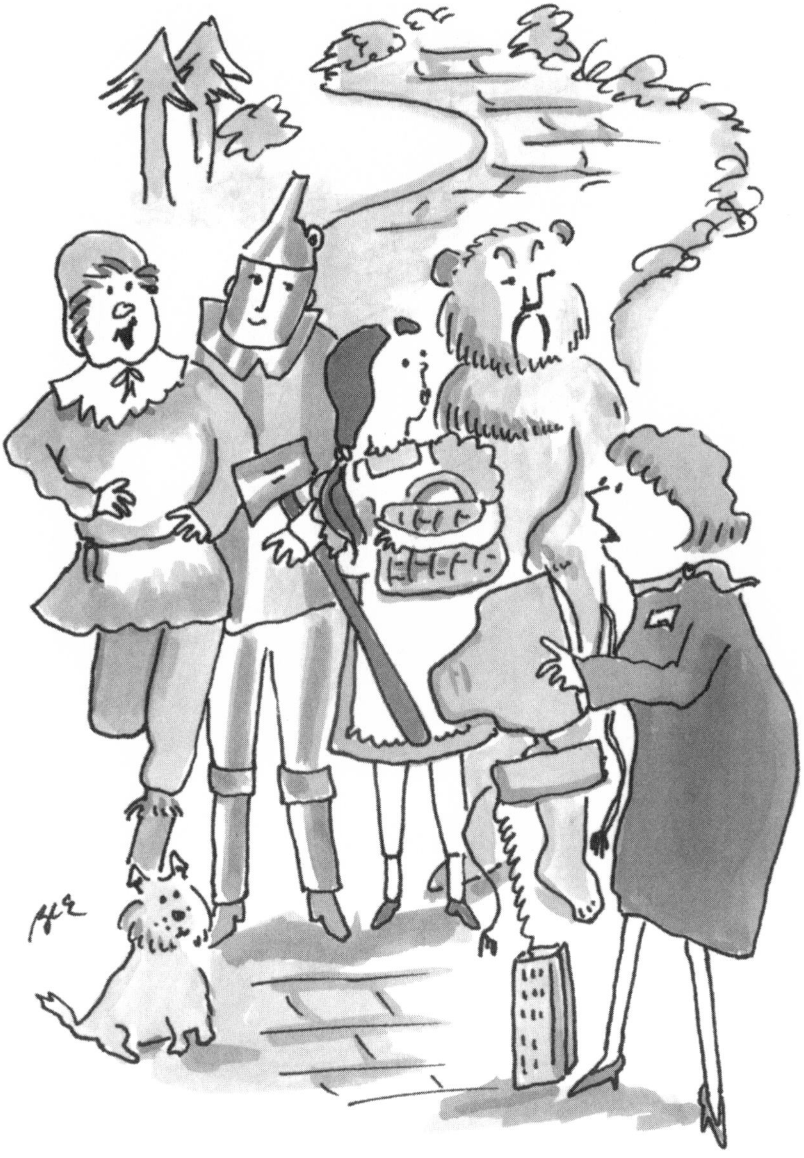

"Can I come with you? My computer needs more memory."

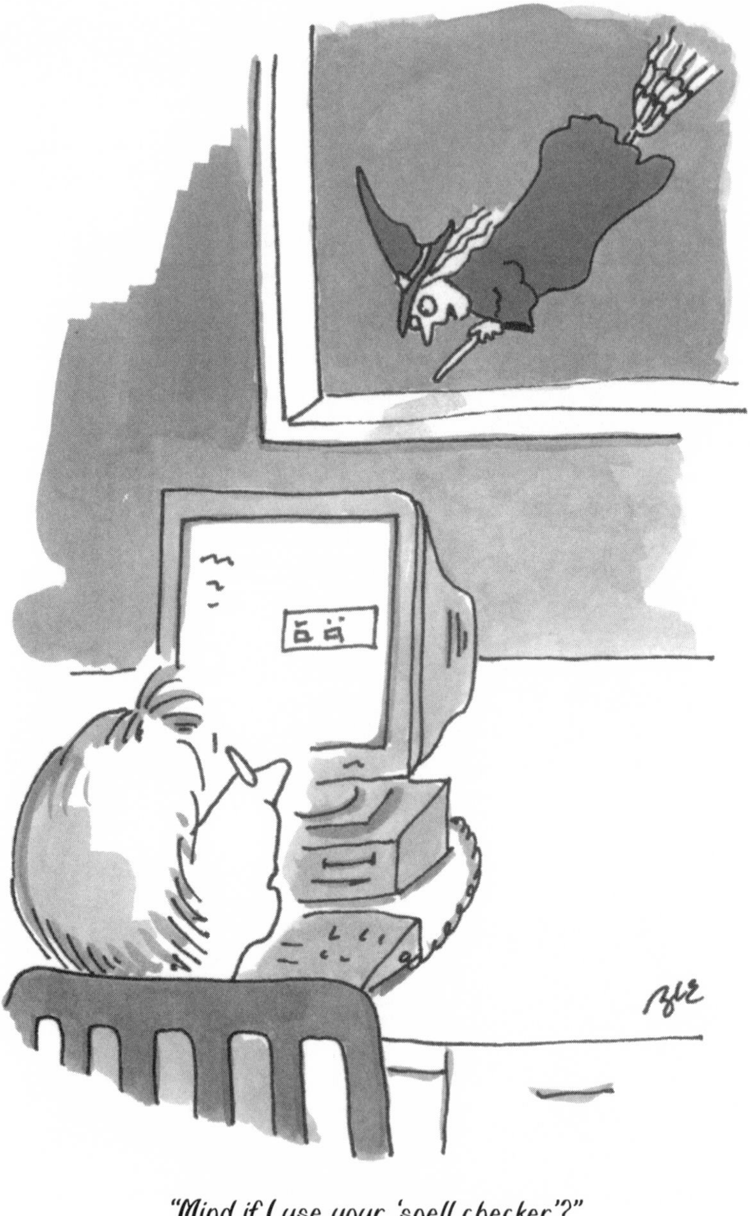

"Mind if I use your 'spell checker'?"

"The library's closing already? But I just
proposed marriage to 200 people online."

"Get help? Sure. What file?"

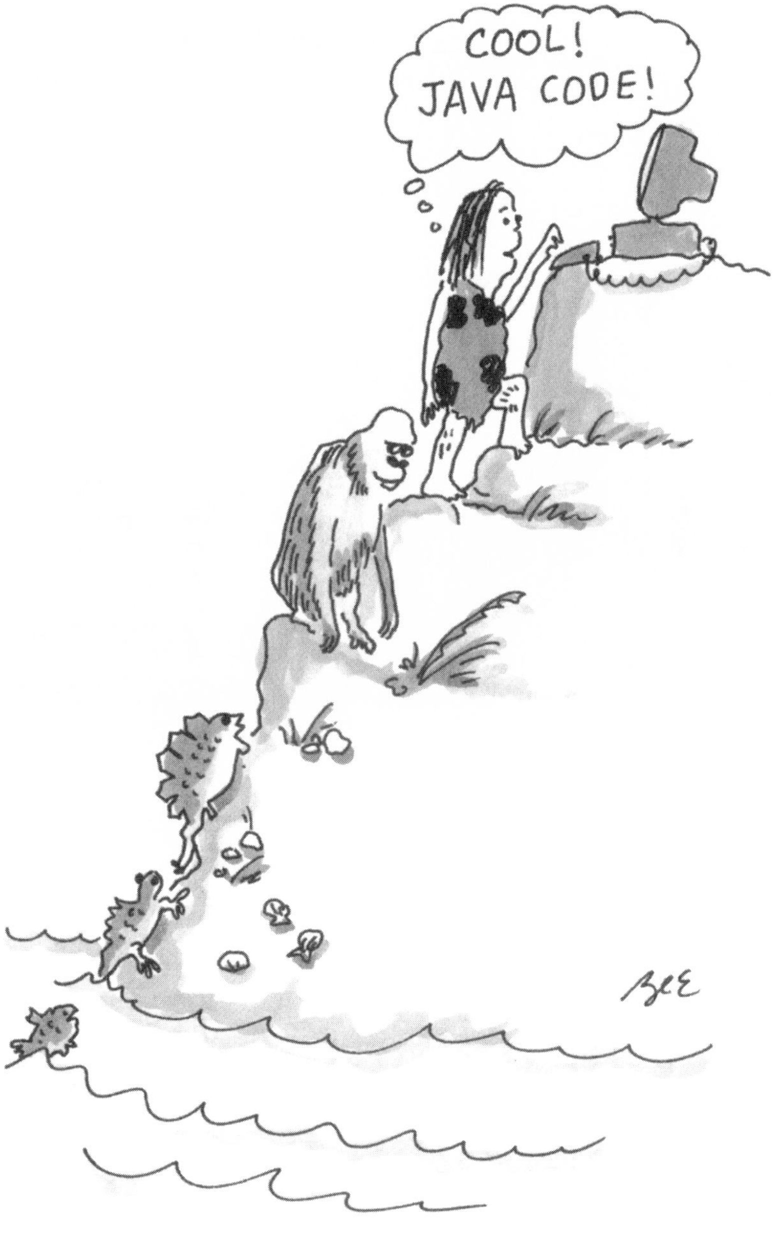
COOL!
JAVA CODE!

"Enjoy your meal!"

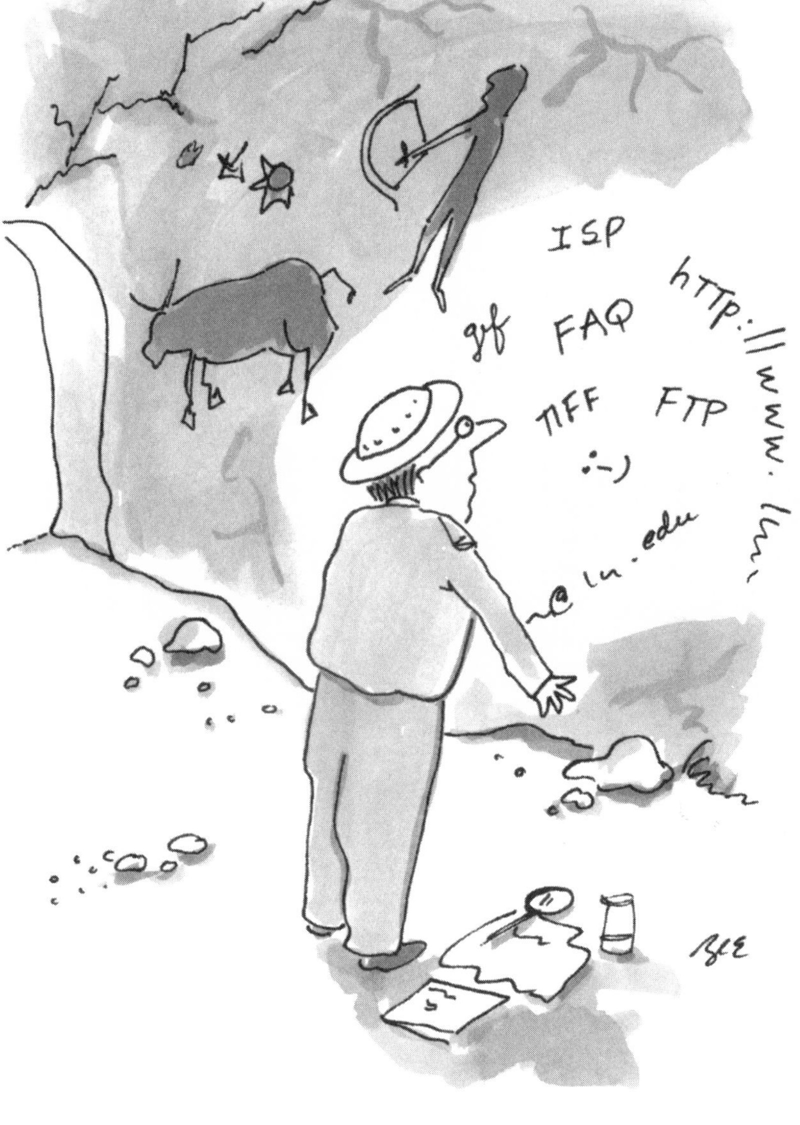
ISP
http://www.
gf
FAQ
TIFF
FTP
:-)
@ iu.edu

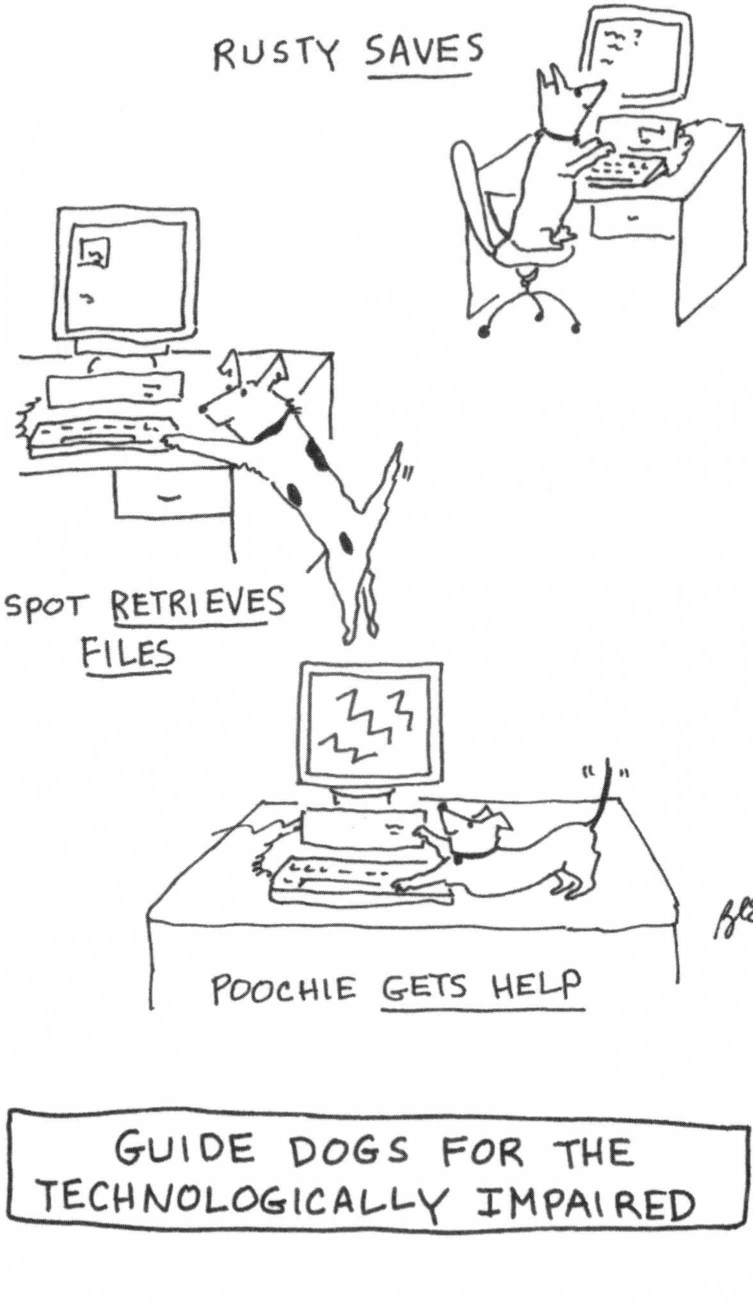
RUSTY SAVES
SPOT RETRIEVES FILES
POOCHIE GETS HELP
GUIDE DOGS FOR THE TECHNOLOGICALLY IMPAIRED

"See? I told you the bottleneck wasn't in the software."

THE DAY THE ENTIRE KEMPLE
FAMILY HAD A VIRUS

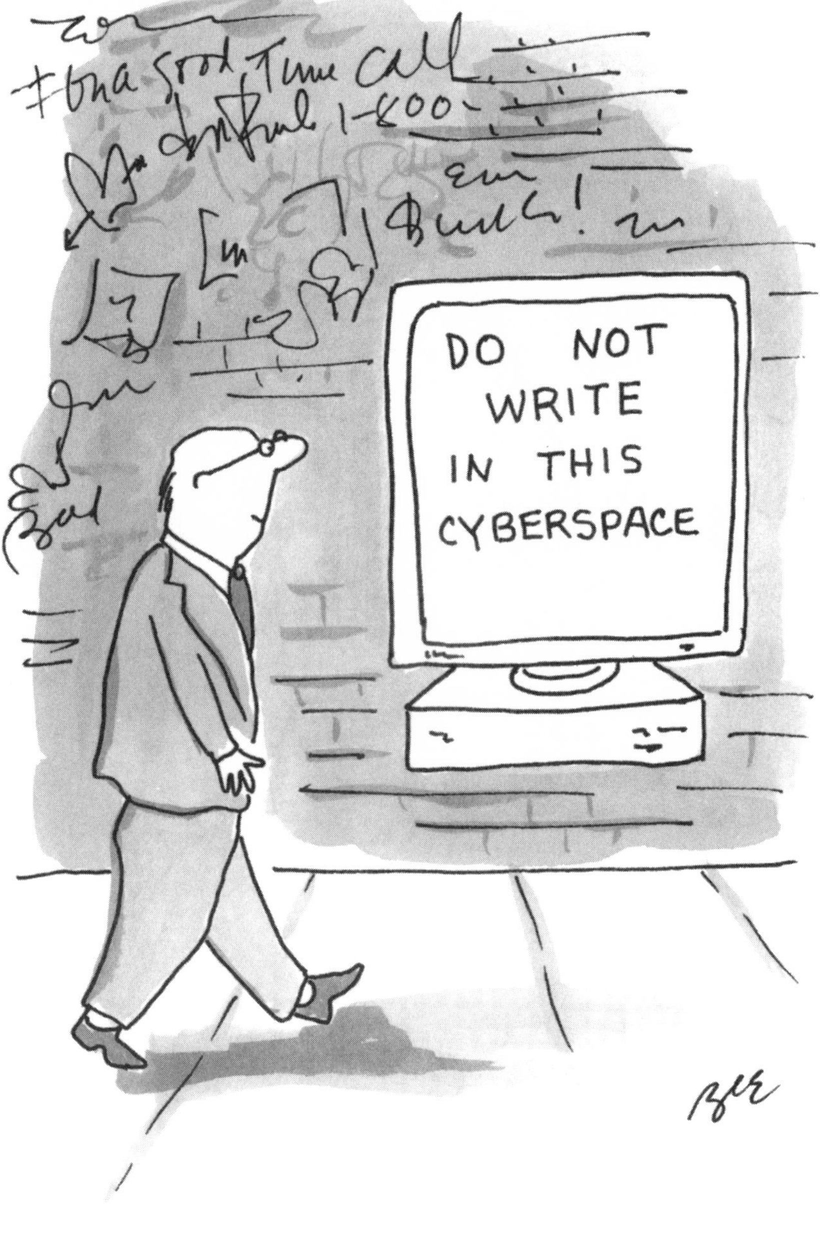
DO NOT WRITE IN THIS CYBERSPACE

"You call yourself a __great ape__? You can't even write HTML."

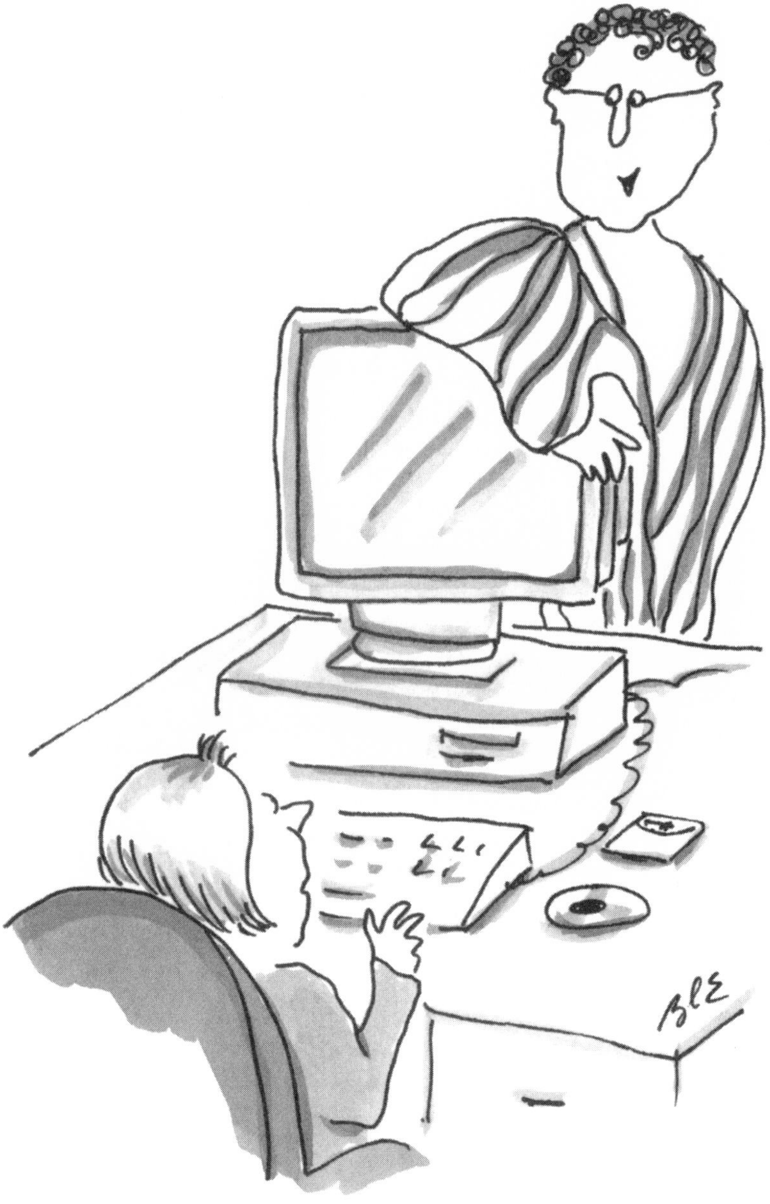

"I am Bracchus, geek god of back-up."

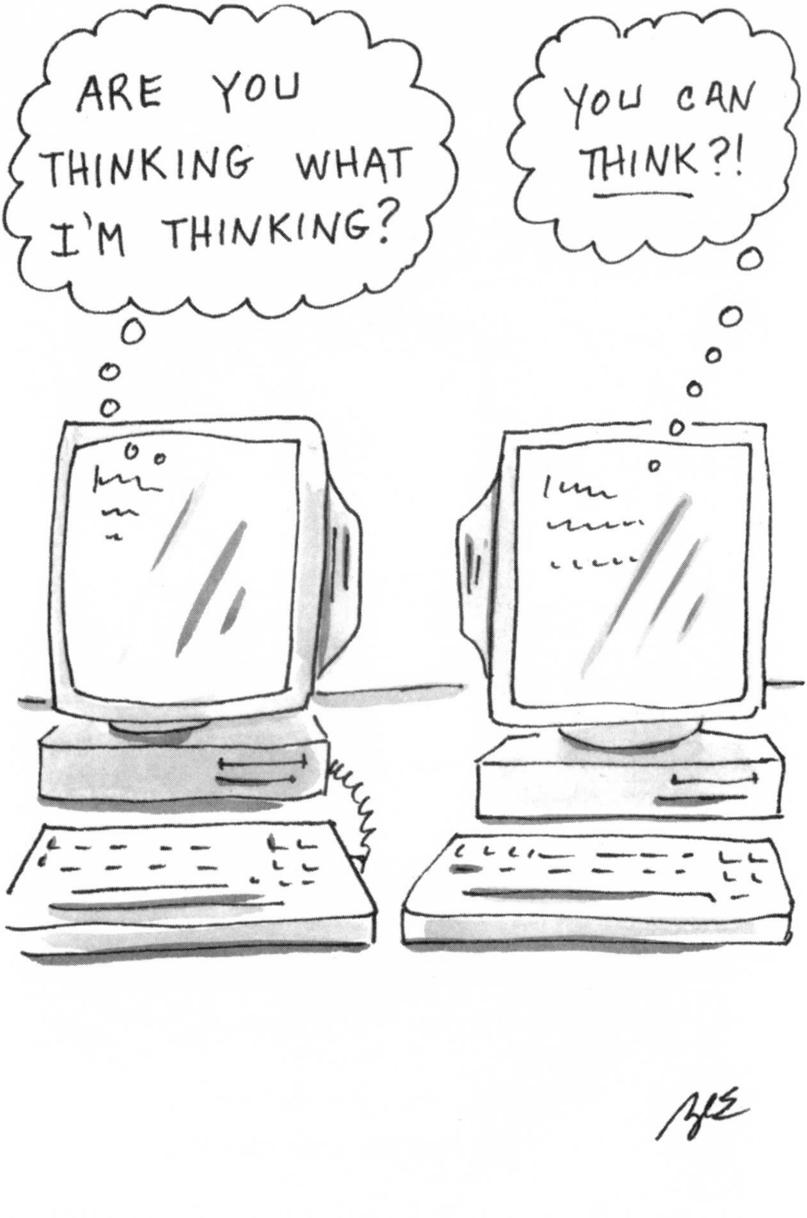
ARE YOU THINKING WHAT I'M THINKING?
YOU CAN THINK?!

"Welcome! You will soon be reunited with all your lost files."

"My name is Jane. I'm a list-serv-aholic."

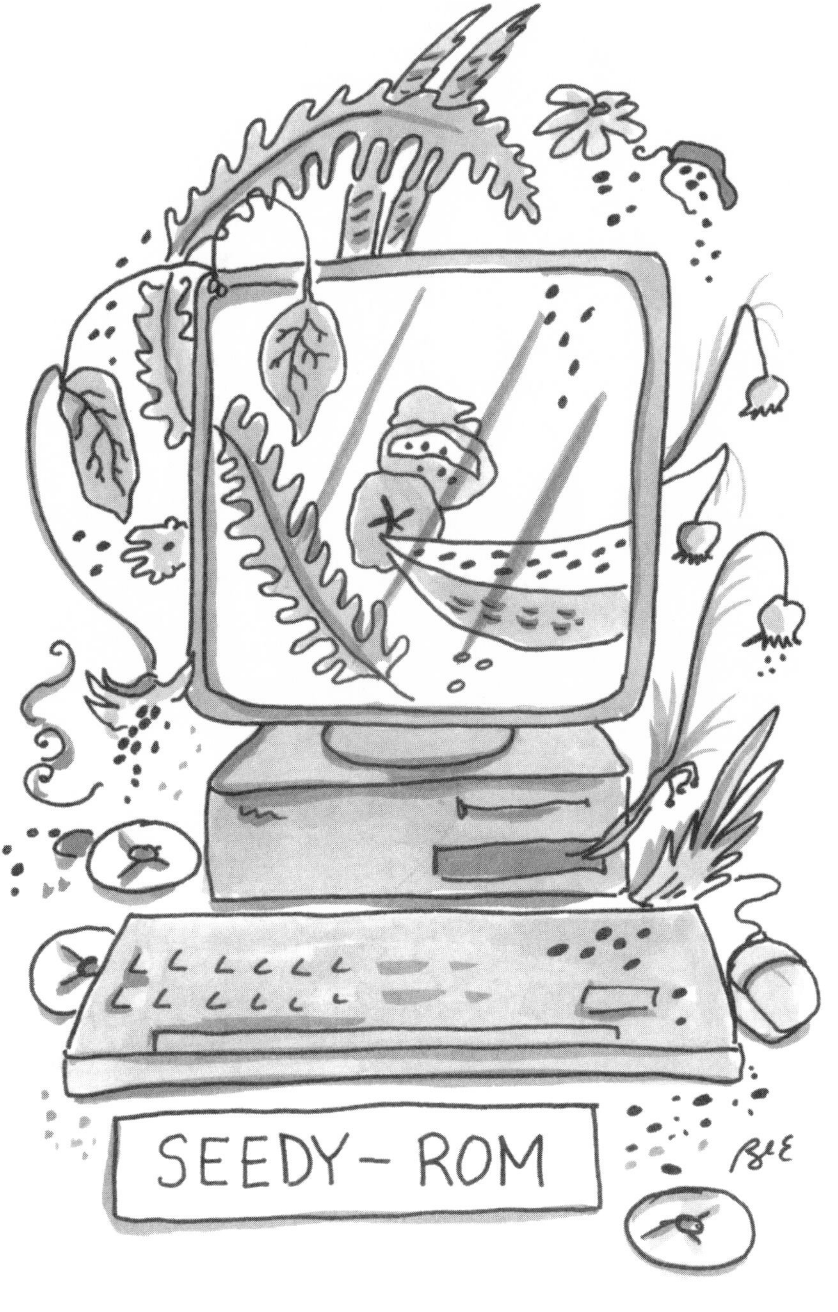
SEEDY-ROM

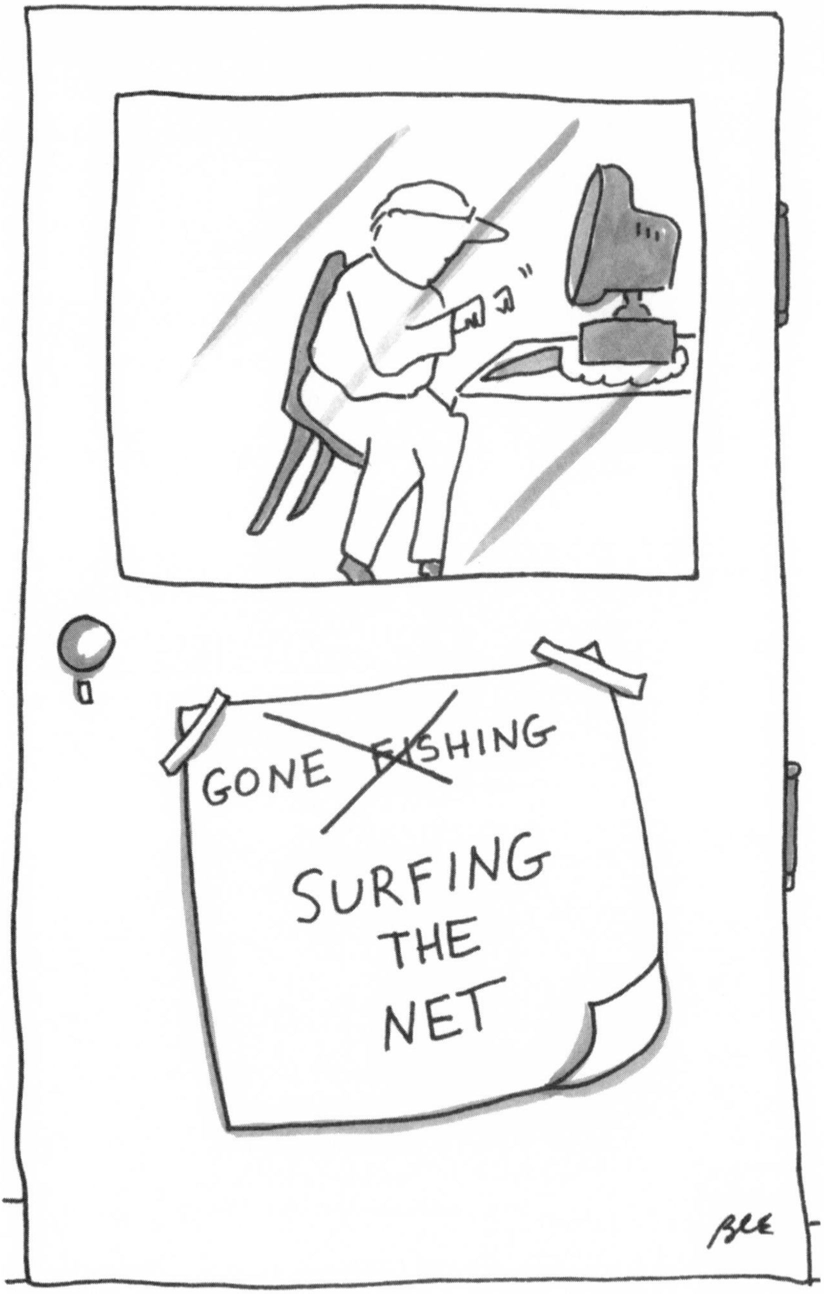
GONE FISHING
SURFING THE NET
BEE

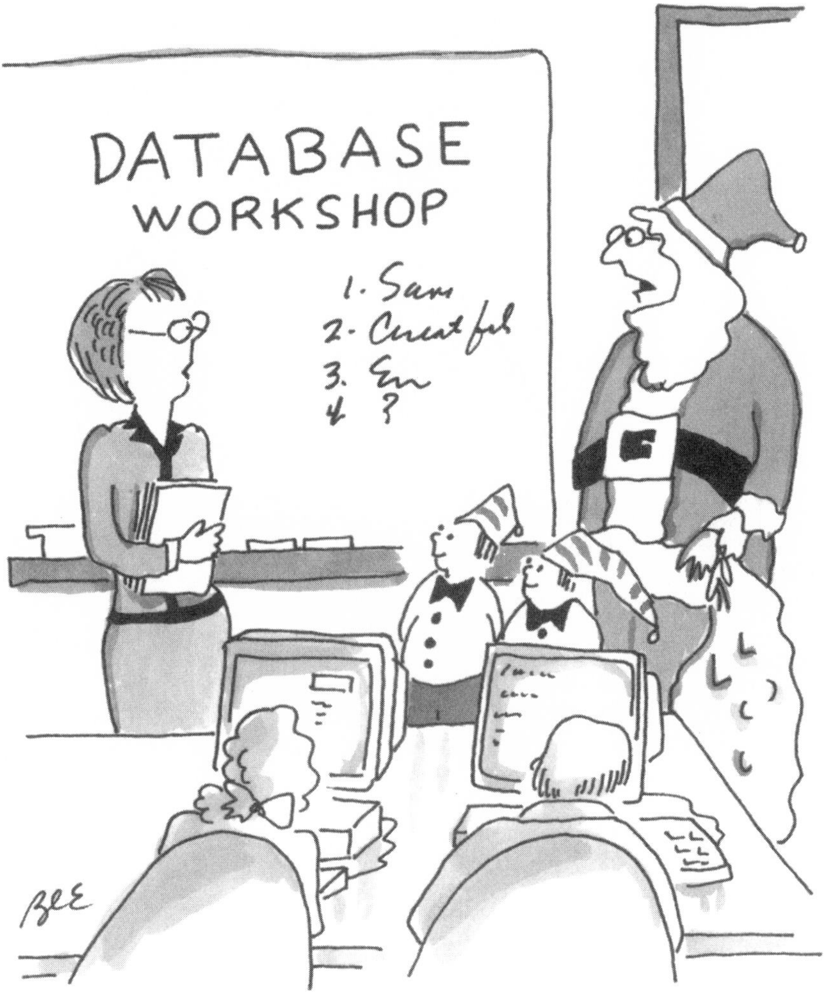
DATABASE
WORKSHOP

"Sorry. Wrong workshop."

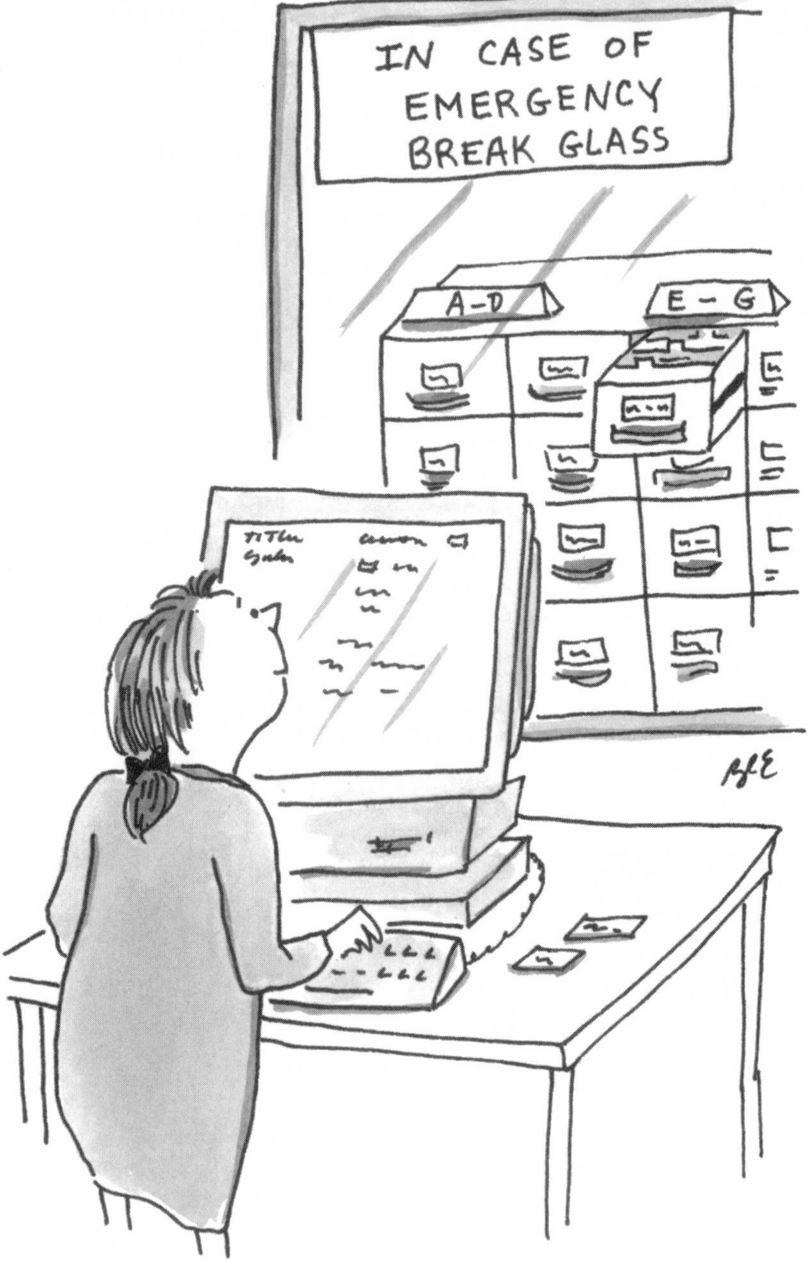
IN CASE OF
EMERGENCY
BREAK GLASS
A–D
E – G

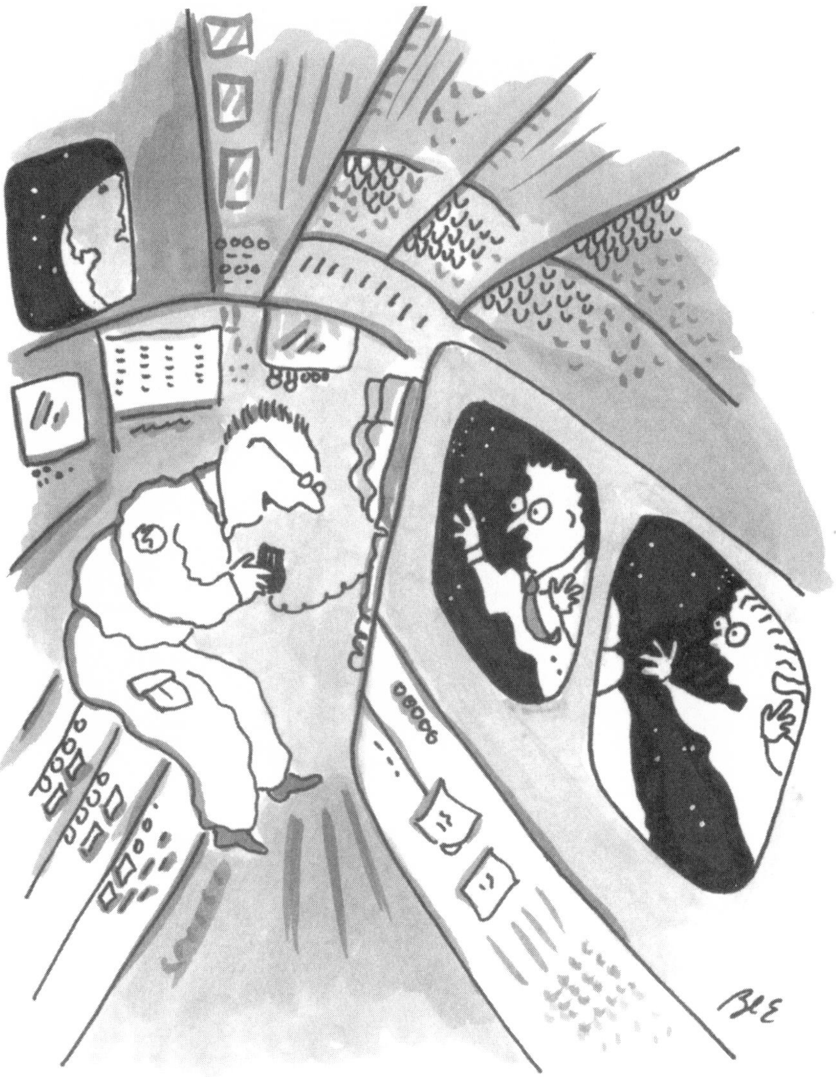

"Mission control? We've got librarians searching the ends of the earth for the perfect retrieval system."

WRITERS, SCHOLARS AND ARTISTS

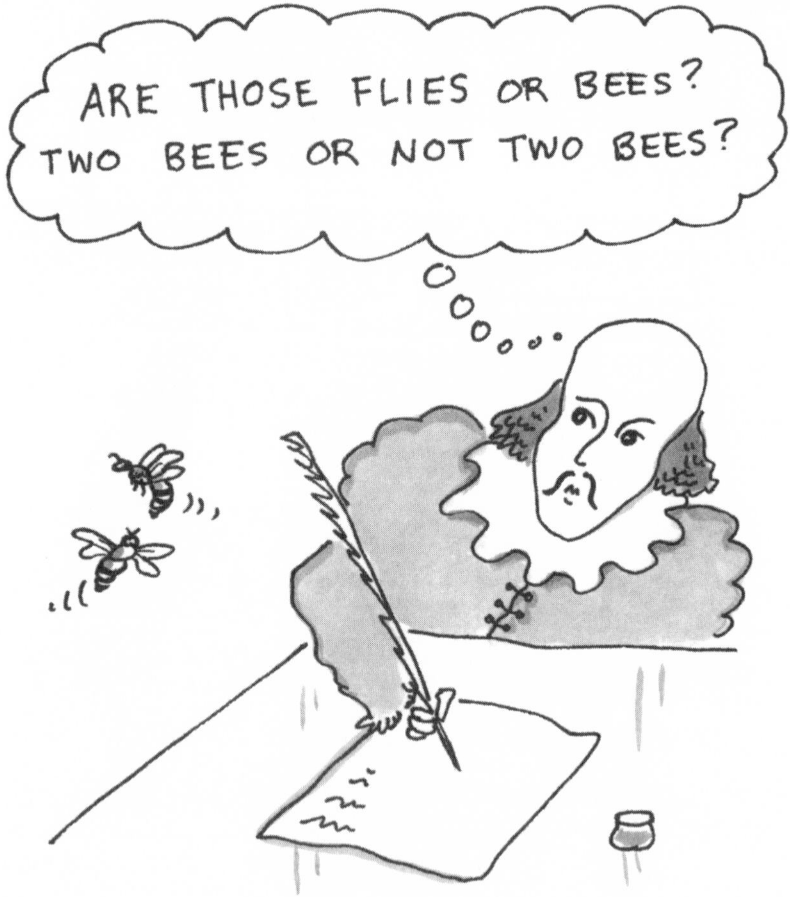
ARE THOSE FLIES OR BEES?
TWO BEES OR NOT TWO BEES?

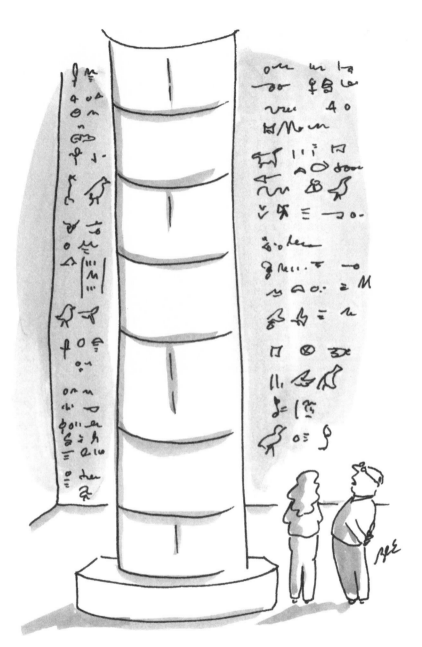

"It says, 'I once knew a man from Nantucket'."

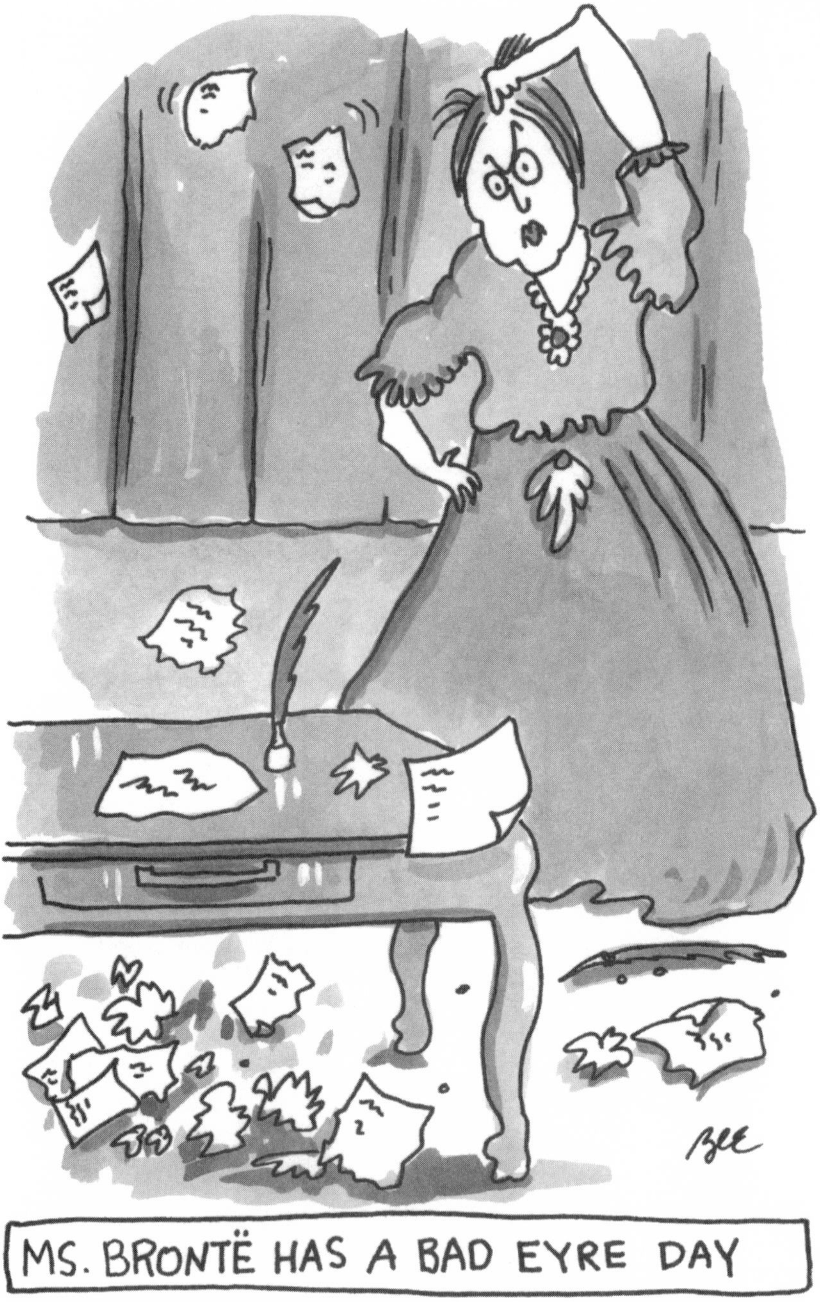

MS. BRONTË HAS A BAD EYRE DAY

FOOD FOR THOUGHT CAFÉ
"MENU DRIVEN"
STRAWBERRY SHAKESPEARE $2.00
TRUMAN COMPOTE $1.50
AESOP SOUP $2.50
TENNYSON VENISON $4.00
GRAPES (OF WRATH) $1.75
BLUE PLATO SPECIAL $6.50

"How do you spell 'procrastination'?"

"Really?"

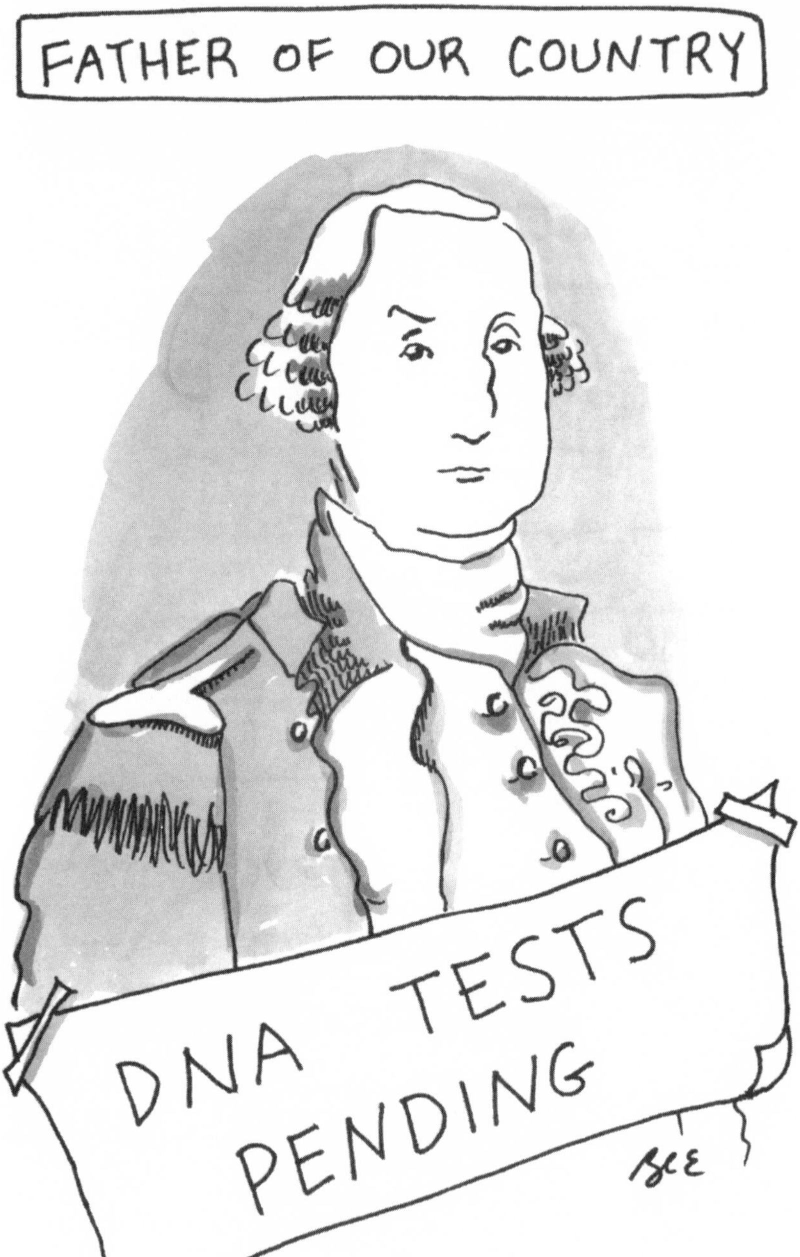
FATHER OF OUR COUNTRY
DNA TESTS PENDING
BCE

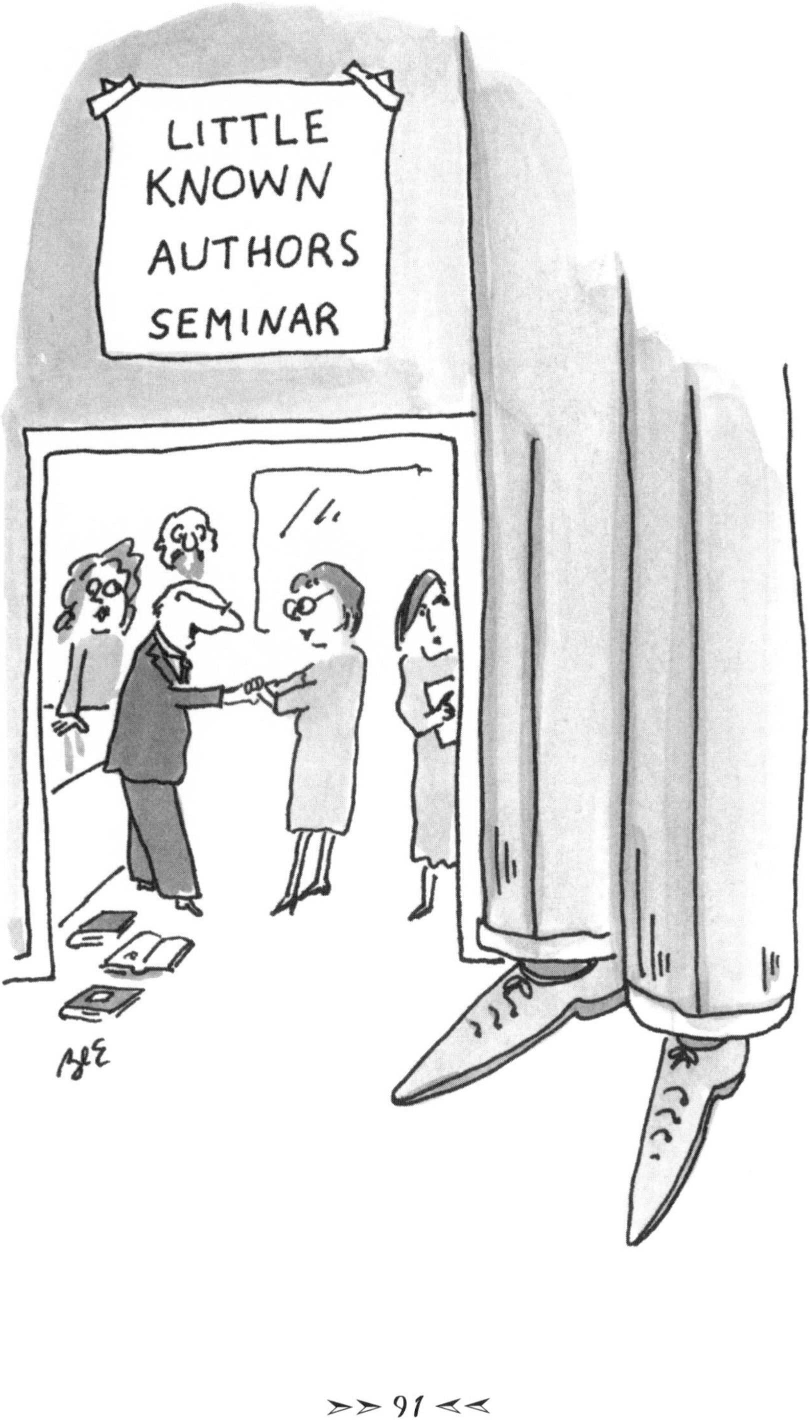
LITTLE
KNOWN
AUTHORS
SEMINAR

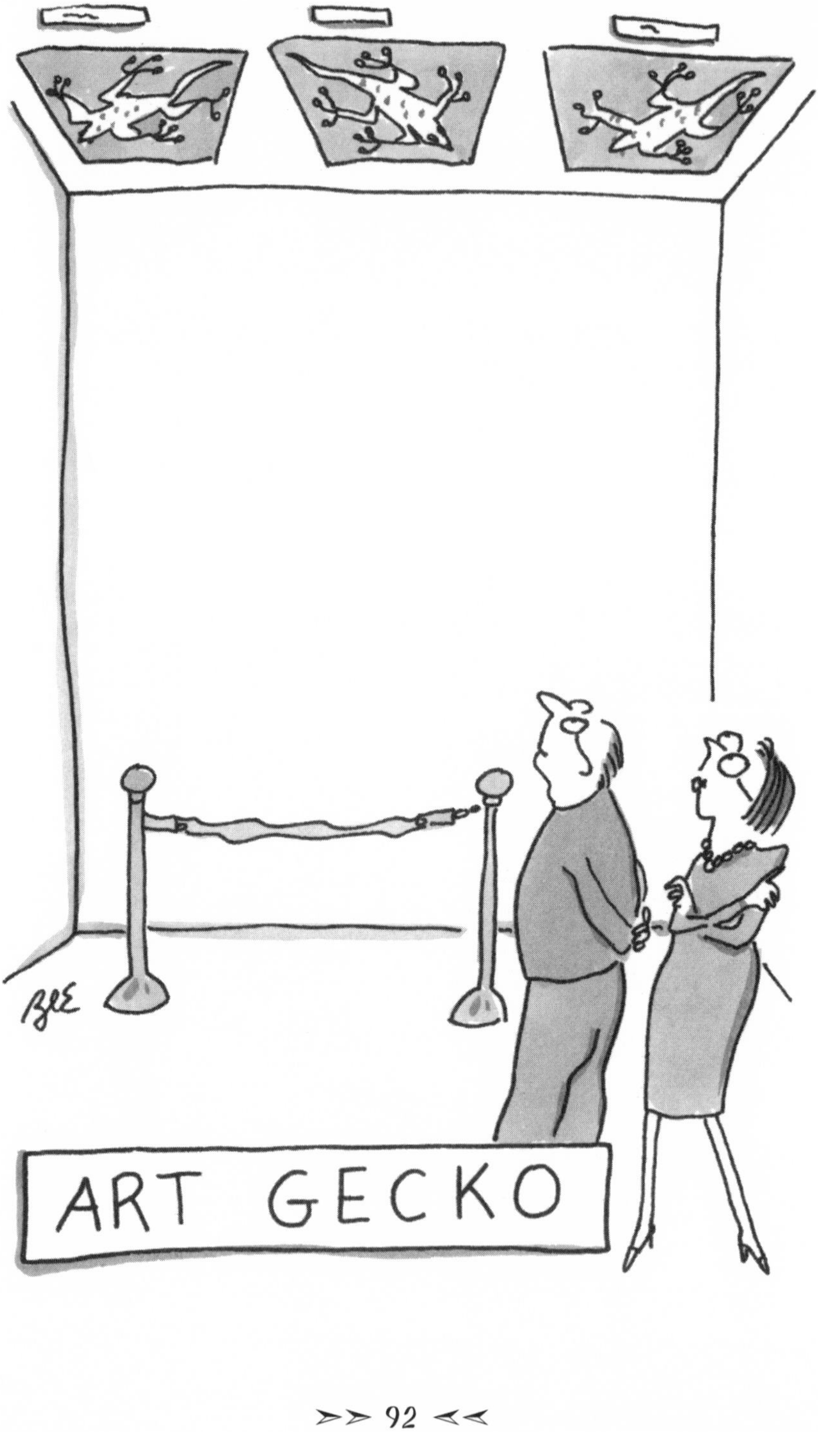
ART GECKO

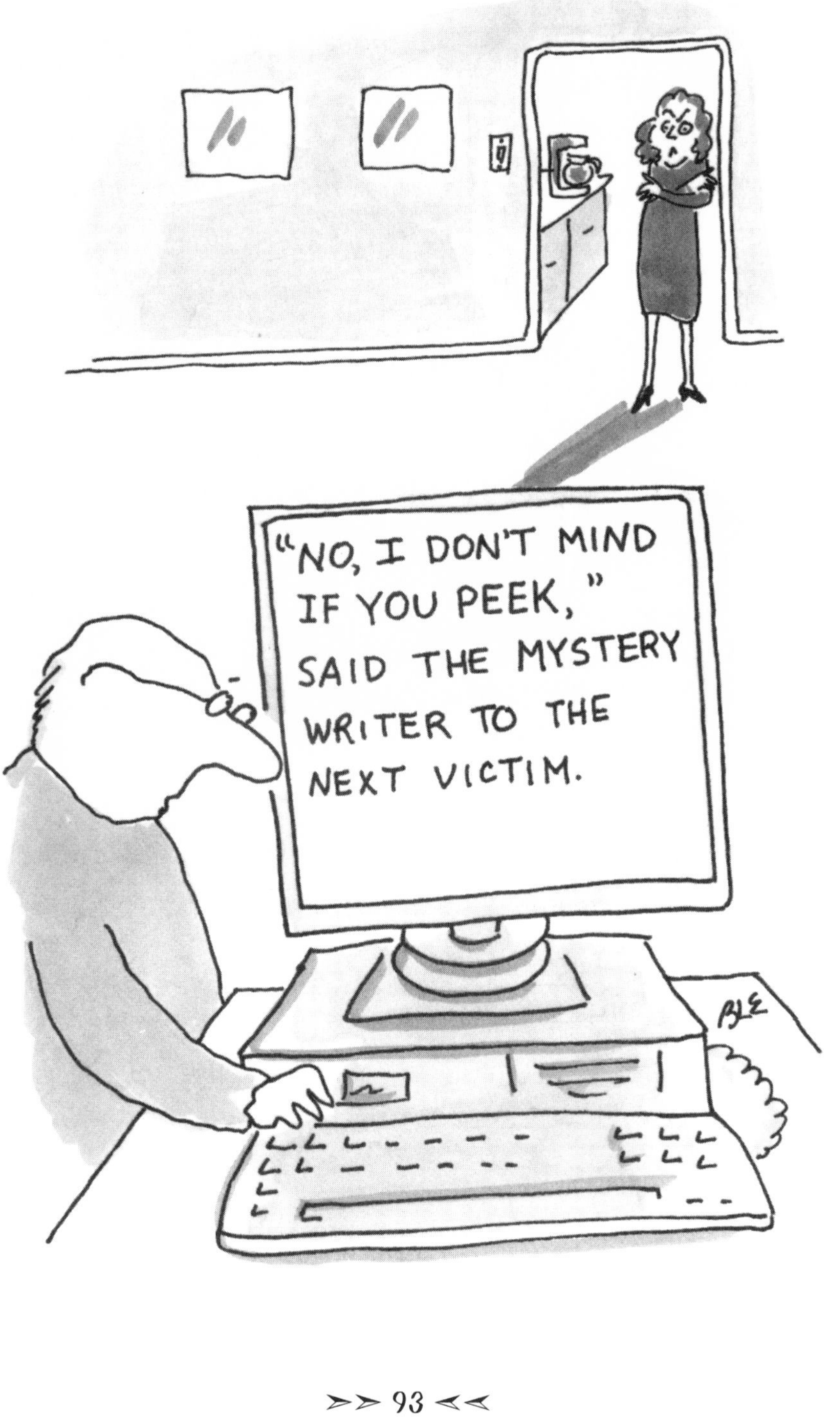
"NO, I DON'T MIND IF YOU PEEK," SAID THE MYSTERY WRITER TO THE NEXT VICTIM.
BLE

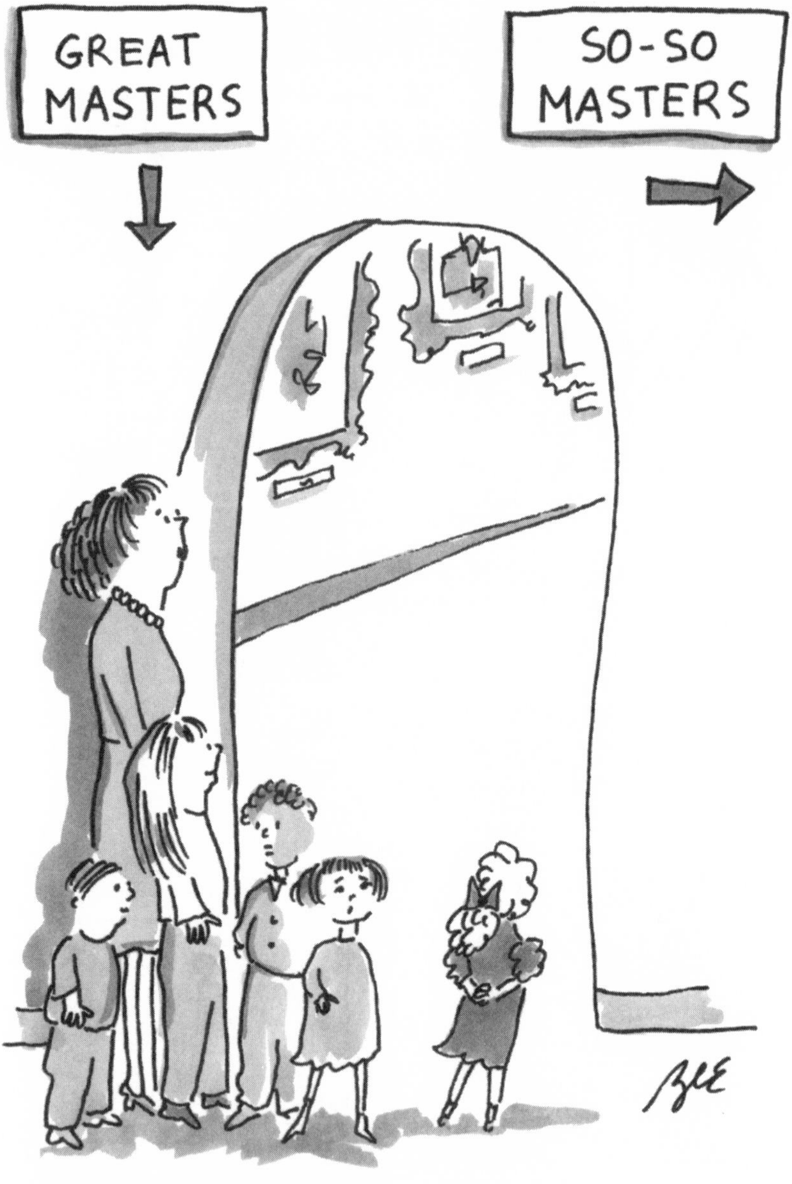
GREAT
MASTERS
SO-SO
MASTERS

THE DAY THEY INVENTED PAPYRUS

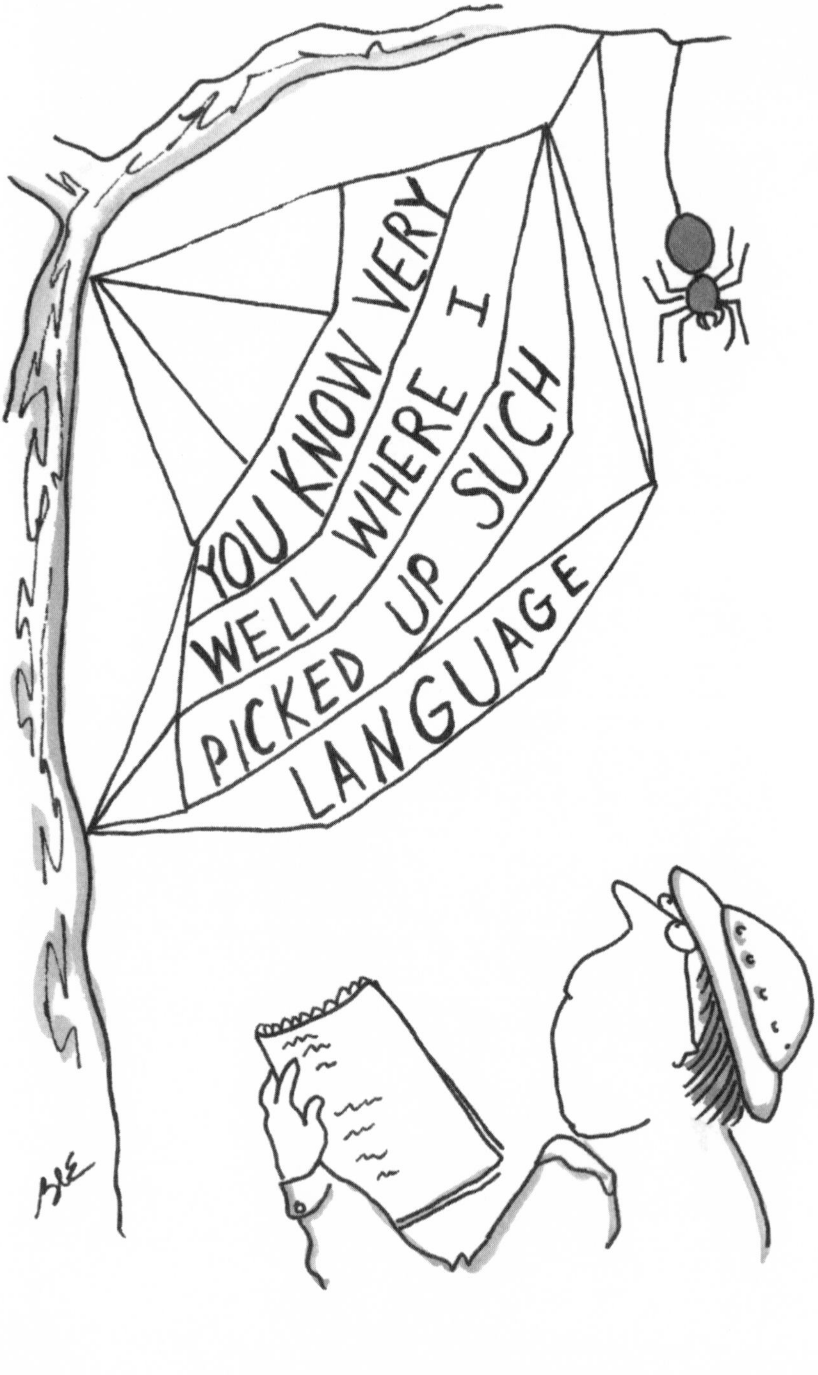
YOU KNOW VERY
WELL WHERE I
PICKED UP SUCH
LANGUAGE

ARTHUR GEORGE
1902 - 1998
WRITER
WHO ENDED
WITH A
PREPOSITION.

"I already wrote the paper. That's
why it's so hard to get the right data."

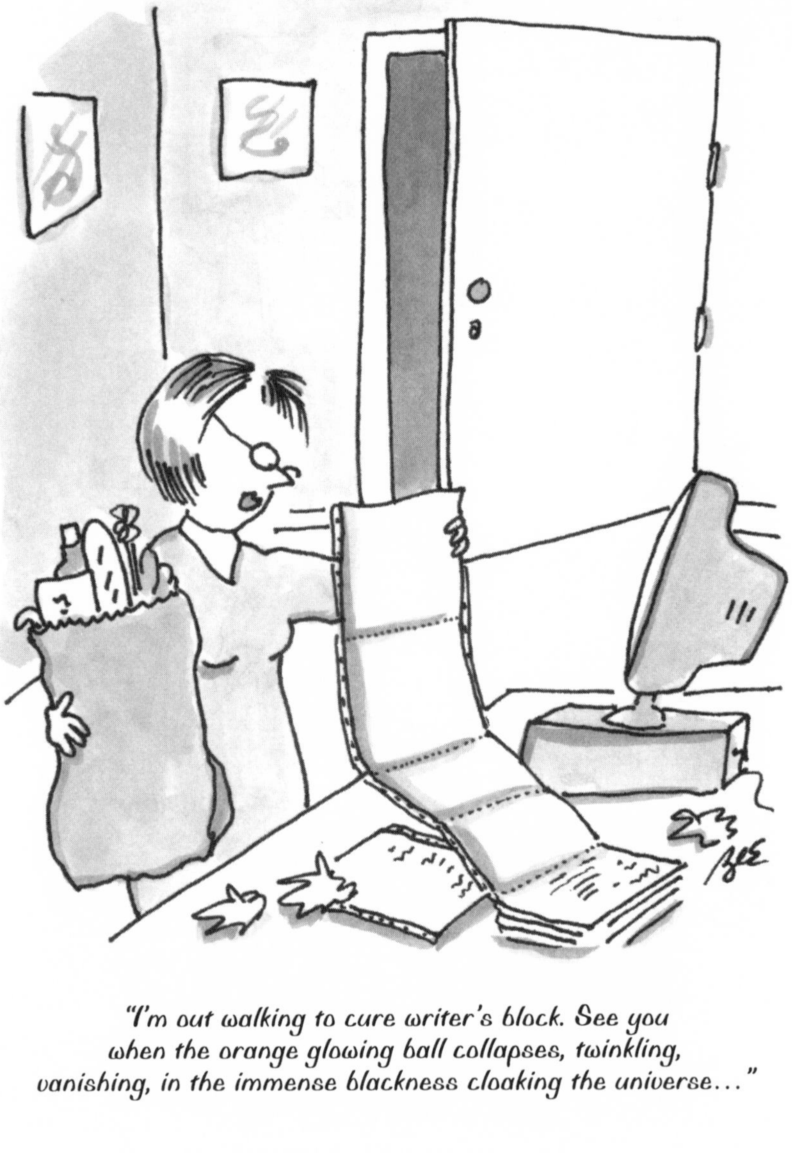

"I'm out walking to cure writer's block. See you when the orange glowing ball collapses, twinkling, vanishing, in the immense blackness cloaking the universe..."

"Yes, Pat Lyons of Seaside, Massachusetts, sitting next to Dale Harmon, class of '58, it _is_ important for a writer to know his audience."

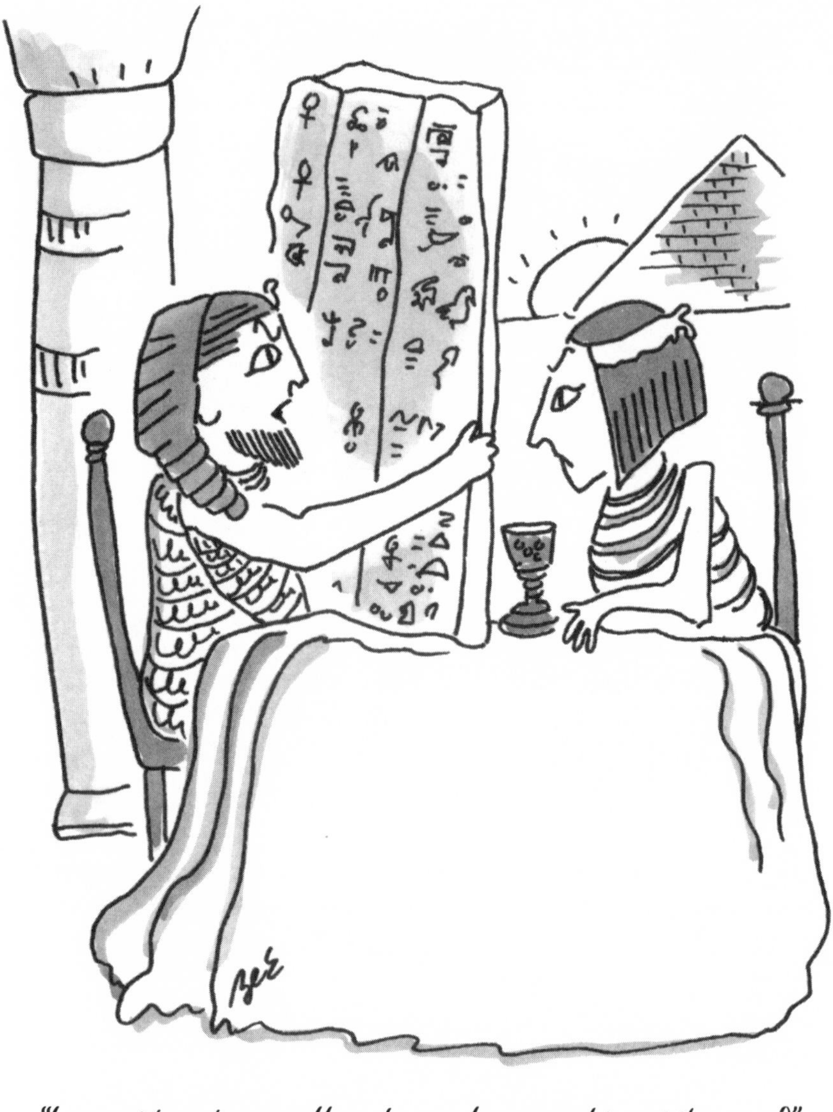

"I am not ignoring you. How else am I supposed to get the news?"

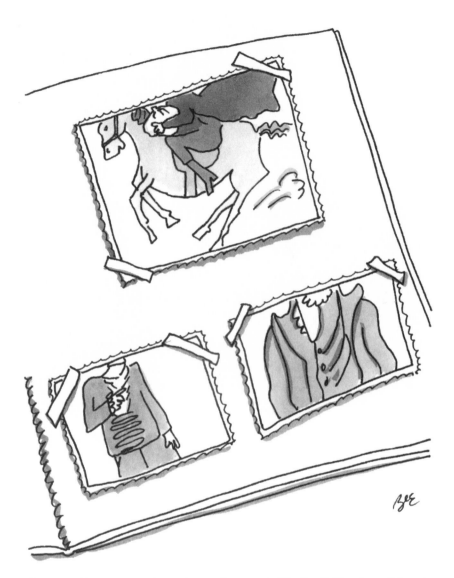

"...then Washington Irving's mother said, 'My God! They're all <u>head-less</u>! Maybe you should try writing instead'."

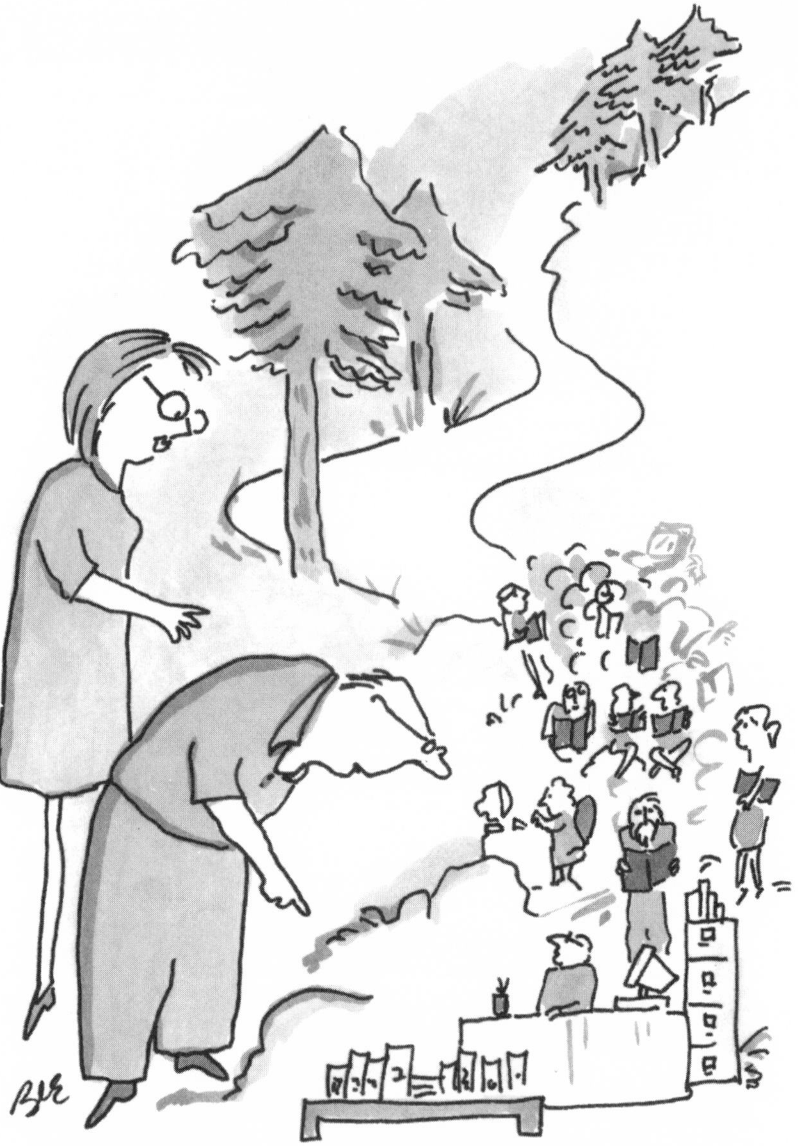

"Did you know there was a little writer's colony out here?"

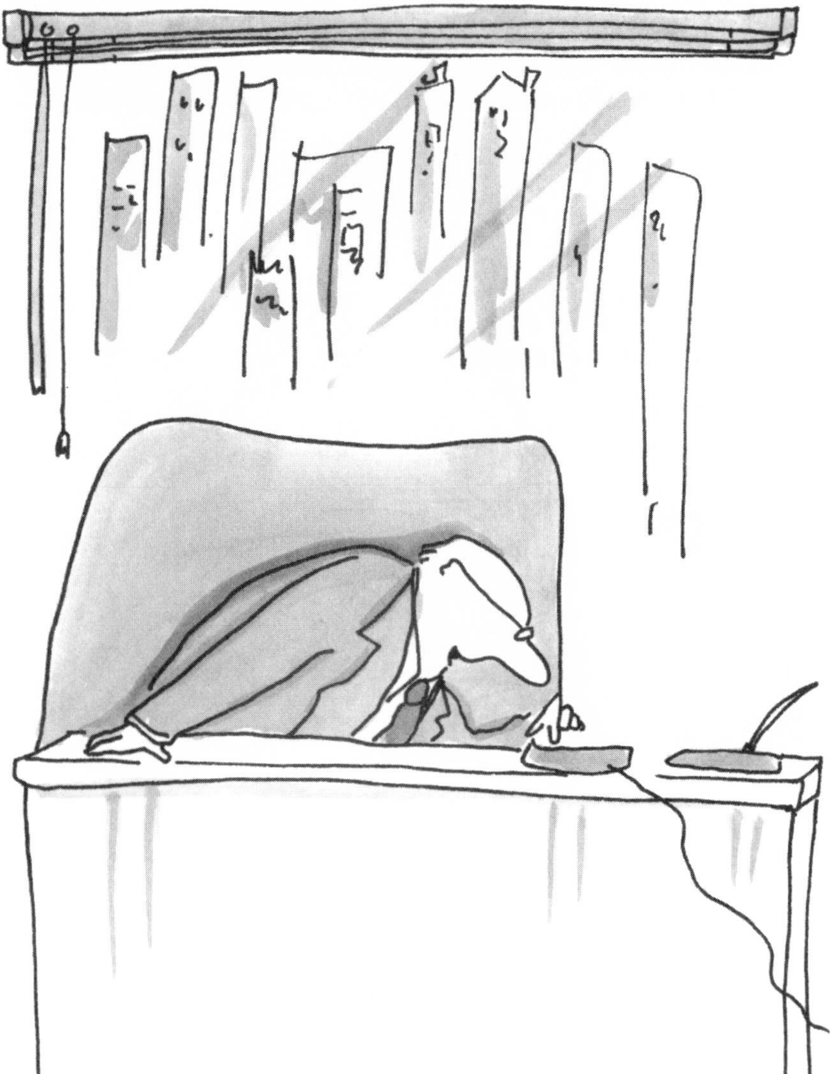
Bee

"I've decided to write a novel, Ms. McDowell. Know any good stories?"

Journal entry. Report on the expedition:
Day 7281. "So far, it's cold as ice."

"This is only a fifty word article. No need to elaborate on your escape from a box."

"That's the introduction to your paper—'Hi! I'm Larry'?"

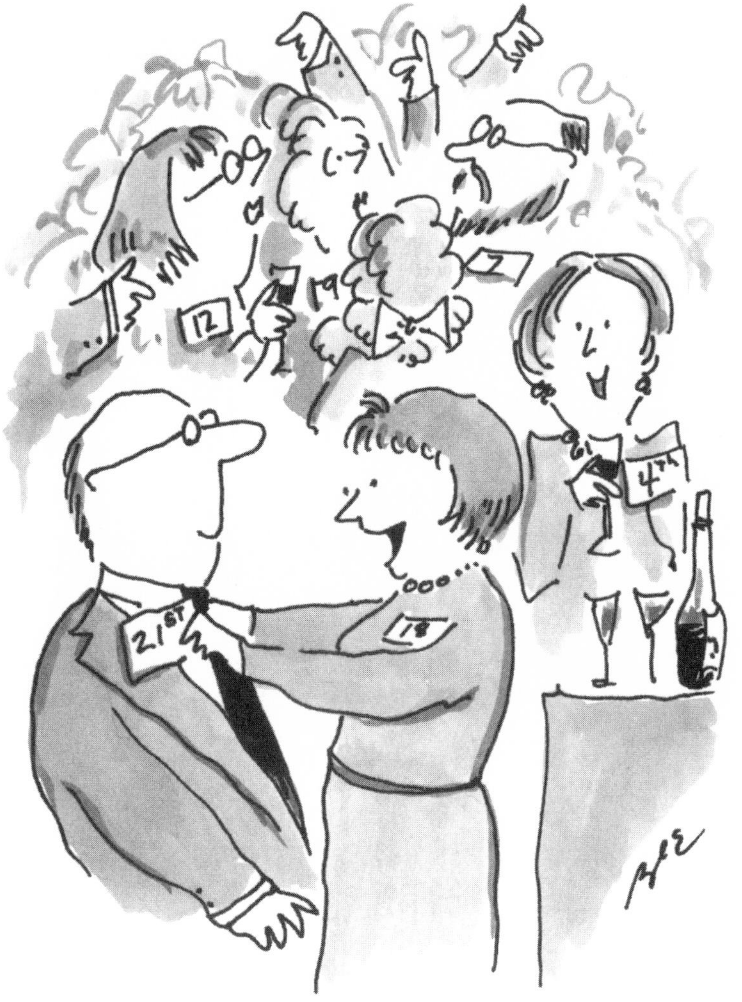
12
19
21st
18
4th

"Welcome to the coauthor's party! You're number twenty-one."

QUIT YOUR JOB AND EARN THREE TIMES YOUR SALARY SENDING JUNK E-MAIL TO MILLIONS OF INTERNET USERS

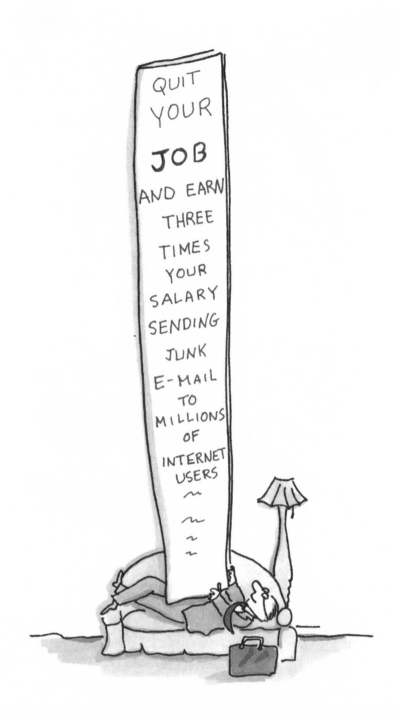

"They say inside everyone there's a writer."